THE THREAD OF MY LIFE
BY LOUIS A. MCKAY SR.

THE STORY OF A MARINE WITH A QUEST TO AVENGE THE DEATH OF HIS TEAMMATE

Copyright © 2016 byLOUIS A. MCKAY, SR.
All rights reserved. No part of this book may be reproduced,
scanned.
Or
Distributed in any printed or electronic form without
permission.
EditonA: January, 2016
Printed in the United States of America
ISBN: ISBN 13-978-1517451332-
ISBN 10-1517451337]

For Information: Wilford Cruz 714-879-7075
wwilcruz@sbcglobal.net
or Buy Book @ Amazon.com

*"What lies behind us and what lies ahead of us
are tiny
matters compared to what lives within us."*

Henry David Thoreau

CONTENTS

Battles I fought, Saipan, June 1944. Tinian 24 July -1
Aug.,1944,Okinawa - April-June 1944, and wounded and
lost my leg. Next step was Iwo Jima February 1945.

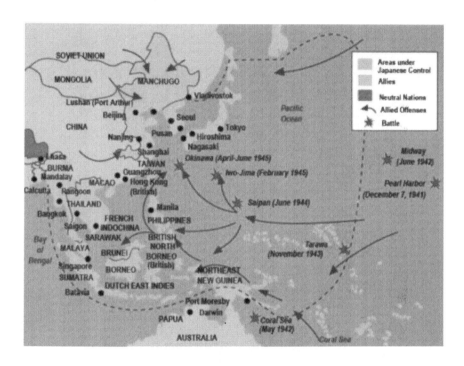

U.S Marines wading ashore on Tinian.

FOREWARD
SURVIVOR OF OKINAWA'S HORROR

Badly wounded by a Japanese shell, Marine spent almost two years in the hospital and opted to have his leg amputated at the knee.

For Louis McKay, World War II was personal.

Raised in Douglas, Arizona, a small town on the Mexican border, he joined the Marines on June 14, 1943, his 20th birthday, after a high school baseball teammate was killed by the Japanese in combat in New Guinea.

"I wanted to avenge him," McKay, said.

But he remembers what it felt like to go into combat, full of hatred and primed for payback.

He liked it.

"I was always happy getting ready for battle," he said. "The quicker we got rid of them, the sooner I could come home to the USA. I was in a deadly mood."

Okinawa was the last and biggest of the Pacific Island battles. It started in early April, 1945, and ran for 82 days. The fighting was particularly fierce because both sides understood that an Allied victory would put it within striking distance for an invasion of mainland Japan. At 92 years of age, he outlived two wives. He has a small apartment in a three-story building in North Park. His grown children, three boys and two girls, live in town. Once a year he goes back home to Douglas to help raise funds for cancer research.

Copyright 2015 - THE SAN DIEGO UNION TRIBUNE
All rights reserved, by John Wilkens, Staff Writer

PREFACE

Sitting back in the warmth of my apartment, I reflect on my life at 92 years and breathe a sigh of relief.

It has always been my belief that one must first take care of themselves before taking care of anyone else. Grateful for my health and the income to enjoy the simple things in life, my goal each day is to go out of my way to do something for someone in need. I don't worry and I have no regrets.

If I had to live my life over again, I wouldn't change a thing. People say that if you don't have regrets, you haven't lived. I believe things happen for a reason and situations will work themselves out the way they are supposed to.

Had I chosen another path in life, it would not place me where I'm at today? I enjoy my life too much to wish that I had made different decisions or chosen alternative paths.

I survived a World War, two tumultuous marriages, put a roof over my head and food on the table for six children, earned a Masters Degree, sustained three successful careers and cared for an additional family.

Each morning, over coffee, I look out onto the city and give thanks for another day. I feel blessed that my family is healthy and doing well. Unfortunately, I've outlived all but a handful of high school classmates.

I reflect on the untimely passing of a very special woman. I remove her floral handkerchief from my pocket and press it against my cheeks taking in her faint *White Diamonds* perfume.

ACKNOWLEDGEMENTS:

Cover Design: Julie Miller

Transcriber: Lita Arvizu

Editors: Wilford Cruz
Rose Clements, Michael Cruz,

Production and Photography:
Wilford Cruz

San Diego Honor Flight:
jeff@honorflightsandiego.org

Publisher: Cruz Publishing Company

THIS BOOK IS DEDICATED TO:

MY MOTHER, MARIA LUISA CRUZ, JOYCE
MCKAY, AND MY CHILDREN, BRADFORD
DOUGLAS MCKAY, LINDA BIRKELAND,
LOUIS A. MCKAY JR., LANCE A. MCKAY,
LISA A. MCKAY, AND LITA A. ARVIZO. MY
BROTHER WILFORD AND JOAN CRUZ, MY
SISTERS, WILMA MILLER,ROSE CLEMENTS.
THEIR CHILDREN, MY NEPHEW AND
NIECES, MICHAEL AND COLLEEN CRUZ.
NADINE BALDSARE, SAM NICO CRUZLORI
TRAVIS, DOREEN,JAWAD, YVONNE,
JACQUELINE, JULIE MILLER, AND ALL
THOSE THAT HAVE HELPED ME BE WHAT I,
AM.   *LOUIS ALEXANDER MCKAY SR.*

Mom Maria Luisa Mckay Cruz & Joyce McKay

Chapter 1 My Mother's Metal Trunk

The journey of discovery began the day my mother's metal trunk first arrived at my apartment. As a young boy, I can recall us struggling to move it, whenever we retreated to a new home. She always had it locked in her bedroom, so it wouldn't be disturbed.

The four-foot high trunk sat unopened in my room for a number of years. At one point, I used it as a side table, and ignored the subtle reminders it would give whenever I would bump into it or have to maneuver my way around it.

A part of me was hesitant to delve into the project and the other part of me was looking forward to what I might uncover. It would be a few years before the two thoughts would collide and a decision was made. I was hoping that the trunk contained redundant bits and pieces of my family's history. I didn't give myself an explanation as to why I waited so long. Perhaps there is a right time for everything I thought.

CHAPTER 2 - Trunk Full of Memories

When I lift the lid to the trunk, the latch is broken, and the metal proves worn. My mother, Maria Luisa Castillo's familiar floral scent is recognizable. There seems to be no rhyme or reason to the vast amount of pictures, envelopes, letters, albums, baby shoes, and newspaper clippings.

The hand-made crocheted and knitted blankets are neatly folded in the corners, along with the doilies. When did she has the time to save all of this and how did she keep track of everything?

My mother helped encapsulate my life and I was about to put the pieces together. I organized the contents as best I could in order to make some kind of a time-line of events.

The first stack of pictures are those of my mother. She was born in Hermosillo, Mexico in 1898. She lived a rough life. But, I never heard her complain. She was always diligent and never sat waiting for a handout.

My mother made me who I am. It is through her that I learned the value of a strong work ethic, and how to treat people.

My dedication and desire to always do something to better myself, is a proud trait that I am glad to say came from her.

Moreover, she's the reason I learned to never say, "No," for an answer. Her motto was to say,— "You appreciate what you have when you earn it."

There are many pictures of my godfather, Manual Alvarez. There are photos of my mother and him together, and the three of us sitting on a porch, including, other photos that covered quite a few years because there were some when I was a baby, a young boy and a teenager. My mother looked happy.

My godfather's nickname was "Nino." He lived in Naco, Arizona. I remember sitting on his front porch, on his lap or down at his feet listening to stories of my mother. It was through my godfather that I learned about my mother and her life as a woman. It was a subject she never talked about. Nino always stood up for my mother and his loyalty ran deep.

Before he would begin a story, he'd put his arm around me and just start talking. He was such a wonderful storyteller; he was soft spoken and gentle. I could listen to his voice forever.

My mother lost both parents when she was a young teenager. Though it was the death of her mother that hit her the hardest – they had a special bond.

My mother had two brothers and two sisters that were killed in an automobile accident, shortly thereafter.

All that was left of the family was mom's older brother Francisco Castillo in Hermosillo, Mexico, and two sisters Cecila Castillo Zepeda, who lived in Naco, Arizona and Herminia Castillo Verdugo in Nogalas, Sonora, Mexico. According to Nino, the brother didn't want mother. He already had a family of his own.

So, mom went to live with her sister, Cecila, who offered my mother sponsorship, thus, she could gain immigration papers to enter the United States from Nogales, Mexico to Naco, Arizona.

At that time, Arizona and Mexico were known as territories not states. It soon became evident that all her sister wanted was someone to cook and clean for the family. Nino particularly didn't care for Cecila since she would order my mother around like a servant.

Cecila wasn't nice to anybody. I remember Nino saying, "She must be a very unhappy person inside."

Since my mother didn't speak of her past, Nino was the storyteller.

There are numerous pictures of my mother in front of the Copper Queen bundled together. The story of how my mother ended up in Bisbee was an interesting one to say the least.

My mother wanted to learn English and make a living on her own so that she could enter and stay in the United States legally. There was talk that the Copper Queen in Bisbee, Arizona, needed a maid. My aunt was not supportive of anything that my mother wanted to do if it meant she would leave.

Who would she get to clean and cook for her? Although they shared words, but it didn't deter my mother's determination.

The next day, my mother walked eight miles, applied for the job and got it. She then walked back to Naco, and packed her bags. I remember Nino saying, "Your mother's adrenalin and anger toward her sister must have been in high gear to walk that distance back and forth. Whatever relationship your mom had it was severed by the hurtful and vindictive comments made by your aunt."

The next morning mother moved to Bisbee. According to Nino, it was at the Copper Queen that my mother met my godmother - Chu Valenzuela. They were close as any two sisters could be. There are numerous pictures of the two of them outside of the Copper Queen Hotel both were chambermaids.

Every picture I picked up had my mother dressed in a black dress and heels. She never wore much makeup.

My mother had heard around town that there was a night school in Douglas, Arizona, for legal immigrants to become American citizens. A woman taught the night course by the name of Josephine Bergner. Pictures of her and my mother are in an envelope.

Mom was the only one in the class that had to commute from Bisbee to Douglas. One day, the immigration office contacted her at work. Cecilia's threats were springing to life; she wanted to revoke mother's sponsorship.

Mother was afraid. She was trying to learn as much English as she could in night school. Hopefully, it would be enough. She met with the authorities, and defended herself so well in English, that they allowed her to continue to work at the Copper Queen and attend night school.

It seems that my mother, even as a teenager, always had the will to fight for what she wanted.

Nino said that Mrs. Bergner admired mother's dedication and desire to become a citizen. One night, after class, Mom was offered a hotel manager position at the Los Angeles Hotel in Douglas. Even though she would move again, she was elated for her new adventure.

This opportunity in Douglas eliminated her daily commute from Bisbee to Douglas. She convinced her best friend, Chu, to come along with her, and together, they would find Chu a job. Shortly, thereafter, she completed her course and at sixteen years old, was an American citizen. She worked at the Los Angeles Hotel for several years.

Pictures of my father Alex, my mother and a marriage certificate are folded in an envelope. Boy! Do I look like my father? I really don't remember him very much because he was never around. He would come by and see me when I was young but it would always upset my mother. So, the times he visited became less frequent.

When Nino would talk to me about my father and the ordeal with my mother, he would shake his head in disbelief.

It was at the Los Angeles Hotel that my mother met my father, Alex McKay. He was the son of her boss — the owner of the Los Angeles Hotel. Alex and my mother dated in secret for several years since it was frowned upon to date and court the hired help.

One day my mother wasn't feeling very well and became nauseous. She went to the doctor and waited a week for the test results. Mom was pregnant. She met with Alex and gave him the wonderful news.

Alex's father was the problem with their relationship they decided to keep everything a secret and were married on October 15, 1922. Alex didn't want to hide the relationship any longer so he told his father he had married my mother and she was pregnant. According to Nino, his father was furious. He called for mom; fired her and demanded their relationship end.

Alex refused and decided to stay with my mother despite his father's orders. Tension had become high with Alex and his father and it started to wear on my mother.

Alex had a womanizing reputation throughout the town. However, when he wanted to marry my mother, she thought that his flirtatious ways would be a thing of the past. Unfortunately, rumors of his infidelity surfaced constantly. He started to come home late and became short-tempered. His excuse was since she wasn't working he had to work harder.

One day, a group of women friends came over and wanted to talk to my mother. They sat her down and told her what she feared all along; Alex has been frequenting the local house of ill repute.

Embarrassed, mom wanted to see for herself. Later that afternoon, she drove over, parked in front and waited for over an hour. All of sudden Alex, threw open the wooden doors laughing with one of his buddies. Mother got out of the car, came face to face with him, and told him to get lost. She felt angry then broken hearted; he had seemingly destroyed her. My father had put her and the unborn baby at risk of contracting a disease. When she returned home, she packed all of his belongings and threw them on the porch.

I remember my mother receiving letters from my father asking her to take him back and give him one more chance. She ignored his pleas, and eventually realized it was not going to happen. If my father had been faithful, perhaps she would have given him another chance.

Alex's father wanted nothing to do with my mother or the pregnancy and my father agreed to be sent away to Denver, Colorado.

During the remainder of the pregnancy, my mother's friend, Chu, moved in, paid the bills, and helped care for her until the time I was born.

CHAPTER 3 – My Birth and Early Childhood

On June 14, 1923, in Douglas, Arizona, I entered the world and was given the name of Louis Alexander McKay. During the 1920s, midwives were fashionable. However, when a woman chose this method of delivery, a birth certificate was hard to come by. My mother wanted to give birth in a hospital, where I was assured of a sterile, safe environment and a birth certificate.

On the back of my baby pictures, in fountain pen ink reads: *Louis Alexander McKay - June 1923.* There are a group of pictures of me wearing what appears to be a satin christening outfit. Another collection of toddler pictures is matted in a circular design similar to what you would purchase from a photographer.

In other pictures I'm dressed in a clean, one-piece knit jumper, *Chipón* (pacifier), white socks and *Choral* (patent leather) shoes. I have a big smile in all of my pictures. I looked happy, clean and well-taken care.

There are pictures of our Hudson Essex Model-T. I'm sitting on the hood in the arms of a woman. On the back reads: *Chu Venezuela – Godmother to Louis – 3 years old.* I remember her like it was yesterday. She was a very nice woman and took very good care of me while my mother worked. She always looked pretty in her dress and high heels. I spent so much time with her that I called her Mama Chu. We'd go for little walks, rides in our Hudson Essex, played games, cards, and went on picnics. We spent everyday together until I started kindergarten at Douglas Elementary. There are no pictures of my father and me.

As a young boy, I remember overhearing my father ask my mother to let him come back. Now that he was a lawyer, he could take care of her. She wanted nothing to do with him. Perhaps, the hurt ran too deep.

Sifting through grade school pictures, I was careful not to damage them. My mother has kept all of my grade school pictures. In one photo, there are ten students and no girls. I'm dressed in a three-piece suit with a lapel scarf. The other boys in the picture are dressed in tattered, dirty overalls. Some are barefoot. Their shirts, pants and shoes display large holes.

It makes sense why I always wear slacks and a tie whenever I go out. Only when it's very hot and humid, do I wear one of my Hawaiian shirts.

Growing up, I never made fun of the other kids, nor did I look down at those who had less then we did. I never saw my mother sitting around and doing nothing. She was always working either as a cook at a local restaurant or at the New Way Laundry & Press starching men's shirts.

As a boy in elementary school, I was fortunate to have two sets of clothing and shoes, one for school and one for play. My godmother evidently began to make decisions for me without asking my mother. This irritated her. It was the straw that broke the camel's back when I called her "Mama Chu" in front of my mother. I couldn't understand what the problem was. I had two mothers. But according to my mother, I had only one, and she was it.

I would see Mama Chu in town, but she was always distant and never talked to me again. I was around eight years old when this happened. Since Mama Chu wasn't around, my mother didn't want me to stay at home alone. I would stay after school and finish my homework in front of my teacher and she would offer to drive me home because my mother worked into the evening.

When I finished my homework, I'd play with both groups of White and Mexican kids. Come dinnertime, the parents of the White kids would call in their children in to eat, but I was never invited. My mother was Mexican. It didn't bother me much, because my mom was probably a better cook.

Since my father's last name was McKay, and my mother's last name was Castillo, I was a "Mestizo" or "half-breed." I didn't belong to the Mexican population and I didn't belong to the American population. I was very proud of who I was. Since my mom worked close to where we lived, she would walk the same route every day. I would meet her half way on the way home and she would buy something to cook for dinner.

As I look back on my childhood, my mother never spoke of the intolerance in Douglas between the Whites and the Mexicans. She never allowed its ugliness to filter into our home. Today, nearly 70 years later, Douglas has its first Mexican Mayor.

While I attended elementary school, I remember helping my mother make ends meet. After school, I would go around the neighborhood and collect empty egg cartons. I would return them to the grocery stores and get paid a penny for each carton. The merchant would then repack the cartons with fresh eggs from the chicken farmers, so they could resell to the public. I would also go through the neighborhoods with my *Radio Flyer* wagon and collect empty glass such as Pabst Blue Ribbon beer bottles. With each full load, I would go to the neighborhood bootleggers and get paid two pennies for each bottle. The bottles were then cleaned and refilled with homemade beer.

During prohibition, bootleggers made beer out of their bathtubs. I was paid well by them and at seven years old, I was making more money than my mother.

Pictures of the Grand Theatre, in Douglas, AZ are scattered throughout the trunk. It was considered to be the largest and most beautiful theatre between Los Angeles, CA and San Antonio, TX. Built in 1919, she is a jewel of southwest architecture and a priceless piece of history. Hand-laid tile adorn her walls and floors. The Grand Theatre has

seen the likes of Ginger Rogers and John Philip Sousa grace
its stage. In the 1920s, The Grand Theatre was recognized
along with those in Los Angeles, CA for movies and shows.

The Theatre closed in 1958 and remained vacant for
years. Due to clogged gutters, the roof caved in and the
infrastructure was virtually destroyed. The theatre has been
undergoing major renovation for the last 10 years. Lack of
funding has slowed down the efforts. However, private
donations, charitable events and organizations have
contributed recently to the resurrection of this historical
landmark.

I remember Mexicans standing outside the Grand
Theatre in food lines with babies crying waiting for their
ration. As I young boy, I walked by the droves of people,
feeling grateful that my mom and I didn't have to be there. I
could go to the theatre with my 10 cents in hand and watch
silent movies.

On days where I would invite a neighbor girl to join
me, I would have to work harder because it would cost me an
additional 15 cents, ten cents for her ticket and five cents for a
Hires root beer with two straws. I would go at least three

times a week, depending upon how much I had left over after giving my mother the money she needed. One afternoon, I remember sitting in the first row and watching a "Talkie" with Al Jolson in the *Jazz Singer*. I found it strange that he was a White man, but he would blacken his face before he would get on stage. After the movie, the audience would enjoy a sing-a-long, "The Bouncing Ball." The ball follows the organ music and tempo of the song. This enabled me to learn songs in English and also memorize them. I would always look forward to singing with the bouncing ball learning songs that were popular at that time.

During intermission, a gentleman by the name of Lowell Thomas, a radio newscaster, would report on the daily news. When he finished his report on President Herbert Hoover, the audience booed. I remember hearing people blaming the President for the depression. I was thankful we had food for our table, and a roof over our heads.

Afterwards, I would return home and share what I had learned with my mother. Looking back, I believe this was the beginning of my love for music.

In the twenties, the street number dictated your status in the city. We lived on 6th Street. In Douglas, people lived in "flats" (apartments). My mom and I rented a two-bedroom house. All the money we earned was put to good use — it was never wasted. Over the years, our savings took the pressure off of daily existence.

One day I came across a box with, *"Louis Alexander McKay's first award"* written in pen. My mother preserved it all these years.

The day the Grand Theater was holding a talent contest for the Mickey Mouse Club, a woman by the name of Louisa Ballesteros, a close friend of my mother, suggested that I learn the song, *"I'm Alone Because I Love You."* This song was very popular at the time. Eddy Arnold made it famous.

On the day of the contest, I remember walking up to the gentleman in charge and giving him my name and the name of the song I was going to perform. They called "Louis McKay" and I performed the song "A Cappella." When I finished, the audience erupted in applause. However, for the contest winner to be announced fairly, the organizer stood behind each contestant. The contestant with the loudest applause would win the contest.

I was presented a 1st place award — a hand-carved face on a trophy of our president, Franklin Delano Roosevelt (FDR). I felt very comfortable singing, and performing in front of people. I think this played a role in how the audience responded.

LOUIS A. McKay SR.
The man behind the mask…many things to many people, and proud to have served with all who sacrificed for our freedoms

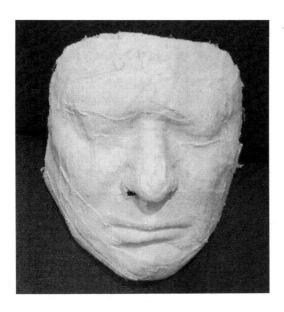

CHAPTER 4-Memorable Moments Of My Youth

There are many pictures of my mother and I, some with Mama Chu and others with a group of her girlfriends. The pictures have everyone posing in front of our Hudson, Essex or Nash Roadster.

One incident that I remember as a boy, was when the Nash overheated in the heat of summer on a return trip from Tucson, we were with a group of women on our way up the mountain to Bisbee when steam came out the front of the car.

In the middle of nowhere, in the hottest heat of the day, and no water, my mother asked the other women what they thought about her survival idea; let the radiator cool, remove the cap, and each woman is to squat over the radiator and pee into it, while the others stood cover to make sure nobody fell off. Seeing this made me want to join in on the fun.

So, I peed into the radiator hole, screwed the cap on, and the Nash started right up. We made it to the top of the mountain and filled the radiator with water at a gas station and continued down the mountain to Douglas.

Later, I picked up the book of my first communion, with the cross and rosary attached. The date read: May 26, 1935. Since I was Catholic, and in order to receive my first communion, it was required that I study catechism at a nun's convent in Douglas.

At twelve years old, my mother and I saved enough money to have a vacation at the Grand Canyon. We traveled to Williams. Williams is situated about 50 miles from the southern rim of the Grand Canyon. It's a popular stop for visitors who want to experience the natural beauty of Arizona. Once my mother realized how much cooler Williams was, in comparison to Douglas, she wanted to stay. She rented a very nice 2-bedroom house. Both of us saved enough money from working in Douglas, thus, my mother could take a break from work and have a little vacation. I chose to work to keep busy.

Since gas stoves were not prevalent at the time, wood burning stoves were used to cook and heat. After school, I worked as a wood stacker. When the trucks would unload the wood scraps at each house, I would separate the pitch (a sap filled piece of wood) from the other wood slabs, and stack and fill each neighbor's barn. I earned two-dollars per barn.

My public grammar school in Williams was as strict as any Catholic school. If kids mouthed off, they were sent to the principal's office and paddled. One day, a girl in the class was bothering me and she would not leave me alone. So, I called her a heifer. I was somehow scared, since I didn't know what was going to happen to me. Would my mother get mad at me? I knew I was in trouble and would not to be able to talk myself out of this. When I reached the principal's office, he said, "Bend over and touch your toes." He had a paddle that seemed to me to be at least two feet long. It was cut out in the middle about four inches. This gave more power to the paddle. I don't remember how many paddles I received, but it was enough that my bottom was sore for days. Later, I found out that the girl was a daughter of a prominent businessman. It didn't matter to me - I would have done it anyway.

Back in my day, parents didn't get involved in the teaching or discipline of students. You treated your teacher with respect — period.

Going back to the trunk, underneath a crocheted blanket are pictures of me as an altar boy in Williams. I chuckle. They bring fond memories.

One Sunday, after church, I heard that the priest was in need of an altar boy. I volunteered and served two masses each

Sunday. One day, after mass, the priest asked me if I would be interested in being his caddy. He offered me 10 cents a round. I told him, "I'll do it for twenty-five."

I was his caddy the next weekend. It was fun getting on the golf course with the smell of the pine trees all around us, a beautiful sky and small patches of clouds, and a cool breeze blowing on us. It was a very refreshing and an exhilarating experience.

As far back as I can remember, I have always tried to make a buck and do everything I can to keep busy. I even helped my next-door neighbor maintain her garden by pulling weeds. Her name was Mrs. Sweetwood. She was always friendly and liked mother and I. She trusted me enough because I was little bit older. She asked me to chaperone her daughter, Babe when she was on a date. She lived part of the year in Williams and part of the year in Phoenix, AZ.

During the winter months there are pictures of me in the snow as a young boy bundled together. On the back, it reads: Louis McKay – Williams, Arizona. The first snow I experienced was in four feet of snow. I woke up in the morning and cars, buildings, homes and trees were covered in a blanket of white snow. I would climb the hills and sled down the sides of the mountains. I couldn't stay out long because I didn't have snow boots.

The leather shoes would get wet and cold and I would have to come in and get out of them to warm my feet and toes over a log fire. Unfortunately, when I had to walk to school, I had to wear my wet boots throughout the day. I also, remember at the same time of the year the heat in Douglas wasn't so bad.

There are pictures of "The Hut" in Williams. This was such a great place to dance. The building is constructed out of pine trees from the mountains and hills of Williams. The interior of the building had built-in wall-to-wall seating made also from the pine trees. It was quite beautiful. There was a stage and bar for the guests to enjoy.

Every Saturday night, the town had a dance at the "The Hut." My mother and I would always attend. The music from the big-band era was fabulous. It was a nice break for me and I soon became a very good dancer. I learned the Waltz and the Foxtrot. I was really happy with our life. My mother and I were content and finally settled.

One Saturday evening, while we were at the dance, my mother met a man by the name of Adolfo Cruz. The minute I met him, I didn't like him. He was not the type of man I wanted for my mother. He drank a lot that evening, and that bothered me. His dancing and charm enamored my mother. She quickly took a liking to him. They saw a great deal of each other and soon she became pregnant. Everything we've worked for all these years flashed before my eyes. Although he did have a job at the lumber mill, he would spend whatever money he had in wages on gallons of Muscatel and Port wine. I soon realized that my mother's situation was going down hill fast, and she was doing nothing to prevent its further demise. One day, I was fed up. I looked her in the eyes and said, "I'm taking a train, moving back to Douglas, and live with my Mama Chu." She was furious. Unfortunately, she moved with me and brought Mr. Cruz with her.

"One incident that I remember as a boy, was when the Nash overheated in the heat of summer on a return trip from Tucson, we were with a group of women on our way up the mountain to Bisbee when steam came out the front of the car." Chapter 4.

Hudson Nash 1926 Roadster

CHAPTER 5-My Life with My Step Father and Siblings

When my mother, Adolfo and I arrived back to Douglas, I was looking forward to serving the church. Perhaps it would provide some peace for a little while. Unfortunately, once the priest found out that I attended public school and not a Catholic school, I wasn't allowed to be an altar boy in Douglas.

I kept myself busy outside of the house with various side jobs. This enabled me to cope with the problems at home. What was so frustrating to me was that I had no voice in how my mother chose to live her life? I felt isolated and had to find peace elsewhere.

Even though we lived in a poor part of town, I always took pride in how I presented myself to the public. The school system in Douglas had a policy where all students in grammar school transferring in from another city, were put back a grade. This had its downfall because when students were put back a grade, I would see them drop out and not return.

Cruz began working for the city, manning a jackhammer to repair the city streets. Eventually, he got a job at the smelter. This enabled us to charge groceries, furniture, or whatever we needed at the Phelps's Dodge Mercantile store. The amount charged throughout a pay period would then be taken out of his paycheck. The problem was that Cruz charged his wine.

On December 10, 1937, my mother gave birth to Wilford Cruz. She delivered the baby with the help of a midwife. When Wilford was a baby, I remember rocking him to sleep singing Lu Lu Que Lu Lu and A La Ru Ri Ru Ri.

These were the melodies mothers and caretakers would often sing as they rocked their children. My mother recovered quickly and was soon up and around. I couldn't spend much time at home with Wilford, as I was busy with work, school and sports.

One day, I saw Adolfo's paycheck lying on the kitchen table, noting: fifty-cents. At the time, our rent was nine dollars a month. Adolfo's drinking problem was getting worse. The money I earned paid the rent, electricity and the telephone.

I was constantly pre-occupied with how we were going to make it. The stress was beginning to take its toll on my studies. I worked every day after school shining shoes for ten cents a pair, and pairing at a local pool hall, and washing dishes for fifty cents a shift at the Rainbow Café. It became harder and harder to make ends meet, so I got another job with Phelps's Dodge, delivering groceries to local residents in the Douglas area.

It was fun because I was out of my element. I was fast and efficient and did such a great job that I did not want to jeopardize it. Mr. Carlson, asked me. "How would you like a job cleaning the floors of the grammar school? Another thing, getting involved in sports will do you some good. There is a high school baseball team practicing right now at 15th Street Park, You can go there now, and while your at it, give him this note."

I ran over a half of a mile to the field.

I didn't know how to play baseball. I didn't even have a mitt or baseball shoes. I knew I could learn the game if someone would teach me. I was out of breath when I arrived. While the Coach was finishing dividing the boys into teams. When Coach looked my way, then, I introduced myself.

"Mr. Carlson told me to give you this note. I'd like to play baseball."

He looked down at my feet and then reached in the duffle bag and gave me a pair of shoes and a mitt. The shoes could fit two of my feet, but I put them on anyway. He threw me a glove and told me to get out in left field.

Practice lasted a couple of hours. To me, it seemed like minutes. I was given the left field position. This was the best thing the Coach could have done for me. I began to learn the game by watching how the pitcher threw the ball, how the team members would catch, hold the bat, position themselves on home plate, and hit the ball. Andy Clinch was a great pitcher and we became instant friends.

When I showed up to the next practice, Coach Thalbert Morrow, gave me a pair of cleats and my own bat with the name, 'Roger Hornsby' inscribed on it.
He shook my hand and smiled, "Welcome to the team."

When I returned home I couldn't wait to tell my mother of the good news and better yet, I had another job. However, my elation plummeted when I walked in the front door. My mother was pregnant again.

I later found out that Mr. Carlson paid for all of my equipment, encouraged the coach to give me an opportunity and paid for out of his own pocket my pay for the custodial job.

At the time, Douglas had one grammar school and one high school. Looking back, the ninth Grade was a turning point in my life. I began to experience sports and competition. I picked up baseball quickly and by the end of the baseball season, I secured the position of left fielder with the nickname of "MAC."

One day after school, a teammate of mine told me that my name had been called earlier that day at an awards assembly at Douglas High School for a varsity letter in baseball. When my name was called, they had informed the coach that I wasn't even a student at the high school, and worse yet — still in grammar school.

When the coach contacted Mr. Carlson and told him of the dilemma, they decided to present me with a letter G for grammar in place of the letter D at the next awards ceremony at my school.

I started my freshman year at Douglas High and I tried out for the Bull Pups - the junior varsity football team. I loved it. I could make a clean hit and tackle as hard as I wanted because it was part of the game. I found that it was very easy for me to disassociate myself from my schoolmates when I was on the field. My classmates wanted me to be their friend on the field and I was there to win a scrimmage and play hard. During my sophomore varsity season, I was asked to replace an injured Varsity Fullback. I kept my grades up so it wasn't an issue. All athletes had to get a 'C' or better in their studies in order to play athletics. After the season, the school awarded me a "d" instead of the "D" for varsity. Being I was a freshman, I didn't have enough quarters on my football record to obtain a varsity letter.

When it came time to try out for Basketball team, I was chosen as a guard. Our three-point distance to the basket was only 2 points. But, I made the baskets. Looking at the team pictures, it shows how the times have changed. The shorts are mid-thigh length. We wore tennis shoes, not the specialty basketball shoes players wear today. My height of 5'8", did not lend itself for me to excel in basketball.

I remember one game against Bisbee. We were two points behind. They had a player, by the name of Graham. He was unstoppable at 6'5." With only a few minutes remaining, I asked the coach to put me in. As Graham ran up to the basket, I fell on all fours in front of him. He ran into me and landed on the other side of the basket and smashed his face against the gymnasium wall. He missed the basket, and we won the game.

At the start of the baseball season, I was already set because I was a left fielder on the Varsity team. One afternoon, I remember when our team went over to the 15th Street Park for practice. The coach informed us that the team's catcher was hit in the eye by softball in an intra-mural softball game. The coach asked for a volunteer to play catcher. I spoke up and said, "I will." I liked the position of catcher. Back in my time, the catcher directed the game and also communicated to the pitcher as to the type of pitch he was to throw — one finger pointed down — a fastball, two fingers pointed down — a curve ball, and three fingers pointed down — a drop. The catcher's mitt is the pitcher's target. The batter is at a disadvantage. He can't prepare if he doesn't know what's coming at him. Home runs were scarce — you had a lot hits.

In baseball, the element of surprise was the name of the game. That's what I liked about it. Andy Clinch and I became a successful battery. I played the position so well that when the regular catcher returned from his injury, later in the season, the coach told him that he was now my backup catcher. With that, the boy quit. By the end of the season, I secured the catcher position.

I am in catcher gear and to my right and behind me is Lew Young and Andy Clinch. (My teammate Andy death was my reason for to joining the Marines…)

CHAPTER 6 – Experiencing High School And Sports

The summer prior to my sophomore year in high school, my mother gave birth to Wilma Cruz on June 19, 1940. In the summer months, it was sweltering, and with nobody to help her during the day, she tired easily.

Adolfo and I were hardly home.

My mother saved all of my annuals, the newspaper clipping from the DOUGLAS DAILY DISPATCH, and the high school newspaper articles from the Border Bulldogs. They all show my dedication to sports, school activities and social clubs. I especially enjoyed singing in the Glee Club. Had no idea that eventually I would follow a career in singing Opera and how technical music was. It was something different.

This also helped me relax with no outside distractions or thoughts, also very inspirational because of the songs we sang.

During my sophomore year, I made the Varsity team in Football. My nickname on the field was Mac – just like the truck. I smile as I glance through the sport section of the Douglas Daily Dispatch:

Trusty McKay took over and with a couple of battering thrusts placed pigskin in clover. (I made a touchdown)

Power driven McKay smacks the herd.

McKay could rate a berth upon any high school gridiron in the State.

Louie McKay – Douglas fullback brought the stands to their feet with a sparkling 45-yard gallop touchdown.

In Basketball, my nickname was Louie and McKay. On the baseball field, I was a catcher — they called me Pepper. I would try to distract the batter of the opposing team by talking the entire time the player was up to bat.

I didn't want to be pigeonholed into any particular ethnic group. I got along with everyone. I avoided conflict. I chose to spend my time and involve myself in sports, social clubs and music whatever job I could get in order to keep money coming in the door.

Pictures of the Pure Food Bakery bring back a tasty memory. I worked there during the summer months braiding dough. The smell of bread baking in the oven was something I never tired of. In the evenings, I would bring home loaves of warm, fresh bread for the family to enjoy with dinner.

In school, the student body, teachers, and coaches knew of me through my actions, how I carried myself and treated other people. My home life was not going to dictate my happiness or prevent me from getting an education and moving ahead in my life. I was so busy studying, working and playing sports, I didn't have time to date, drive in car clubs or socialize much.

I always took pride in my appearance. School mates and teachers alike, had no idea of my home life, and that's the way I wanted it. I had to be in the mindset to make everything outside my home, positive and productive. One day, Coach Morrow, offered to drive me home after school. When we drove up to my flat, the coach looked at me and said, "I had no idea you lived here." I thanked him for the ride and glanced into his eyes, "I'll see you tomorrow."

The evenings when I didn't have to report to work, I finished my homework and helped my mother feed and rock the babies to sleep. When I'd start to sing, it wouldn't be long before they were fast asleep in my arms. I would sing "A La Rurirui" and "Lu Lu Que Lu Lu." These were old Spanish folk songs handed down through the generations. I remember Mama Chu rocking me to sleep singing the same songs.

I never paid attention to the words of "Lu Lu Que Lu Lu." It's such a nice song when you don't know what it says. In

English it's translated, "If you see a mouse come out of the floor, kill it in one blow and throw it in the alley." Imagine we all went to sleep hearing this charming little tale.

During my junior year in high school, I continued to excel and letter in Football, Basketball and Baseball. Newspaper clippings from the DOUGLAS DAILY DISPATCH recount the play-by-play accomplishments of the Douglas Bulldogs. As I read through them, I was a Mac.

McKay is vicious and deadly in his plunges for yardage. McKay plunges through the line giving the Bulldogs the lead. It was the hard driving plays by McKay, which ripped the opposing line to pieces.

Girls wanted to date me, but I didn't have the extra money and I didn't want the problems that came along with dating. The girls that wanted to date me would have their mothers invite me over for hot fudge. I don't know if this was a ploy to get me to date their daughters, but I would always be cordial and thank them for their hospitality.

I would often have to do my homework during lunch. After school, I had sports and then off to work in the evenings.

I got a job as a ditch digger and helped build the Douglas Airfield for the US Government. One day, on the way home from work and after the job was complete, I noticed a truck full of workers that worked longer hours and obviously made more money. I stood in front of a truck, flagged it down and asked the driver where they were going? I told him I needed a job.

The driver said, "If you're foolish enough to stand in front of a truck and ask for work, you've got the job."

I was paid $90 a week as a Surveyor. My responsibility was to map out the space of the airplane hangers. I would rope off the dimensions of the hangers that housed the airplanes. When the lumber arrived my job was done. So, I asked to be a carpenter's helper. When that job was complete, I went searching for another one.

One day, I was walking in town and noticed a truckload of workers. Bob Corley, a football buddy and classmate was recruiting workers for the Darnell Ranch. I asked him if I could come along. The ranch was located on the outskirts of Douglas. I had no idea what I would be doing, and I didn't care. It was over a weekend, so the timing was perfect.

When we reached the Darnell Ranch, we were told our job was to hoe and remove the locoweed from the cow pasture. It was very important to remove the weed so that the cows would not graze on it and ruin their milk.

There was a barn on the property where the helpers ate and slept. I remember asking Bob Corley where he was sleeping and eating. He was joining the Darnell family in their home. I asked if I could join him and I did. The rest of the stay, I ate and slept in the family home. In the mornings when I would report to work, the other boys would snub me because I didn't join them in their quarters. When the job was finished, we were trucked back to Douglas and paid.

I also had another part-time job as a stock boy at Kress's Five and Dime. My job was to replenish the merchandise according to the manager's stock requests. Each department had their order sheets and I filled them without error. I also would help out in the office adding up the sales receipts for that day.

When that job was finished, I returned to Phelps's Dodge Mercantile, this time as a stock assistant. I would help the store clerks in the attic as they replenished the women's clothing department. When that job was finished, I worked at

Newberry's Five and Dime, as both a stocker and a clerk's assistant.

Pictures of me at Fort Huachuca are faded but bring back a host of memories.

At the end of my junior year in high school Mr. Carlson called me into his office and suggested I apply to the Citizens Military Training Camp at Fort Huachuca in Arizona. The training camp prepared men for Officer-ship in the United States Army. Mr. Carlson, a retired captain in the Army, sponsored my application for admittance and gave his personal recommendation. Once my application was received, the physical examination at Fort Huachuca was scheduled. It's mandatory that all applicants be physically fit and in good health.

On June 13, 1941, my mother gave birth to Rose Cruz. With three kids all under the age of 5, my mother had her hands full. Hopefully, Adolfo would someday realize his help was needed now more than ever.

When my letter of acceptance arrived, I was elated. It stated that I was to report to Ft. Huachuca, Citizen's Military Training Camp. The day I arrived, I received my fatigues, undergarments, socks, shirts, shoes, bedding and toiletries. Then, I was given all of my equipment and assigned a tent with 5 other trainees. The Training lasts four weeks. Your room and board at camp is paid for by the United States Military.

I enjoyed the discipline. I learned to follow orders instantly. This differed from civilian life, in that you don't ask why. You do it because you're ordered. I learned to field strip, clean, load, fire a rifle and a handgun, and have it ready for inspection at any given moment.

My favorite part of the camp was learning how to shoot both a rifle and a handgun at the firing range. Since firing arms were weapons to kill, they were never loaded and fired outside the supervision of your Sgt.

My assigned Sgt. was in the United States Army. He was a sharp shooter. He squeezed the trigger and hit a bulls-eye every single time. I remember my basic training and packing for the three-day/three night survival trip in the Huachuca Mountains.

My Sgt. taught me how to pack a survival kit, which consists of an unloaded rifle, a bandolier with cartridges of ammunition, and a poncho to protect me from the elements, a canteen of water, sea rations and a compass. What I packed had to sustain me for all three days.

This training is designed to teach the importance of rationing water and food during a mission. During this survival drill, we were not allowed to load our rifles or shoot at anything. During camp instruction, everyone is taught to march in close order drills with synchronized steps. I listened to the drill instructor's orders to, platoon halt, platoon forward march, to the rear, oblique left, right or halt.

I remember the first day of marching like it was yesterday. We didn't know our left foot from our right. Some boys collided; rifles clanged into each other, while others went in a totally different direction. It was like a Chinese fire drill, right out of the Keystone Comics. We'd have to march for 50 minutes in close order drill and then rest for 10 minutes. Close order drills teach you to march in step and obey instantly. It's designed to transform and train each individual to perform cohesively and survive as a unit.

The physical aspect of the training consisted of an obstacle course. You had to run, jump over ditches, climb over walls with ropes, and crawl under barbed wire, that was no more than

24 inches in height above the ground. By the end of camp, I was in peak physical and mental condition.

At camp graduation we marched in review before the Governor of Arizona and other dignitaries. We stood at attention as the blues received their Second Lieutenant gold bars. Recruits would receive their stripes when they return the following summer. At the start of the second tour, recruits are given a red stripe, third tour, and a white stripe and at the beginning of the fourth and final tour, a blue stripe.

At graduation, all four-year recruits are given gold bars that indicate a rank of a Second Lieutenant in the United States Army. Once you are given your bars, you are active United States Army.

In order for me to receive a red stripe, I would have had to return the following summer once I graduated from high school.

Association with athletics kept me in contact with my sports buddies. If there was a part-time job in town, I heard about it.

When I started my senior year at Douglas high, I was in the best shape of my life — strong, lean and mentally sharp.

This enabled me to excel in any sport.

There are numerous clippings from the DOUGLAS DAILY DISPATCH recounting my senior year as Fullback. Herman Simon, a buddy of mine, is mentioned throughout the newspaper. We then developed a friendship off the field.

Herman Simon

CHAPTER 7 - The Death Of My Baseball Buddy

I wanted to work and until the day I returned to the Citizen's Military Training Camp. On that day, Herman and I showed up for a job racking balls at the local pool parlor. We decided to split the six tables so we could rack them faster and make more money between us. The men played for money. So it was to our benefit to work fast. We made about $180/week and split it.

The week before I was scheduled to report to the camp, I read in the DOUGLAS DAILY DISPATCH that my baseball buddy, Andy Clinch, was killed in New Guinea, fighting the Japanese in the National Guard. I had heard news coverage over the last year, about how the Marines annihilated the Japanese.

The mindset of a Marine is to "Take No Prisoners." They had a reputation for quality training and achieving goals regardless of the costs of lives. A Marine is not a serviceman he's a warrior and the first to fight our country's battles. The majority, if not all, of the radio and newspaper coverage dealt with the European Campaign: the war against Italy and Germany. Douglas was an Army town, so there was very little coverage made to the Pacific Campaign against the Japanese after Pearl Harbor. This planted a desire in me to join the Marines Corps.

Herman wanted to join the Air Force. He wanted to fly all over the country. However, I talked him into enlisting with me as a Marine, where he could do some real fighting.

My mother wasn't very supportive. She was afraid that I would be killed.

The day I met with the recruiting officer, he told me that I needed to supply three recommendations, one from a teacher, a coach and one from the superintendent of the school district. Once I received all three recommendations, I submitted them to the Marine recruiter. I was on the schedule to enlist the following week. Things were moving very fast but I was happy. At 20 years old, I was looking forward to a new thread in life.

I remember going to visit Mr. Carlson before I left Douglas. I told how much I appreciated his support. Through him, I enjoyed and excelled in sports, stayed in school, received my diploma, and took an active interest in the military.

The next week, Herman and I boarded a train and headed to Bisbee, Arizona, along with the other new recruits from all the branches of the military. I remember being so elated to be leaving Douglas and all the problems that I lived through for so many years. It was in Bisbee that we were officially sworn in as a Marine. Each was given a choice of either Paris Island, South Carolina or San Diego, California, for boot camp. Herman and I chose San Diego. Right away, we hopped on a train and headed west.

I remember the minute we set foot in San Diego. There were representatives from all the branches of the military to meet their respective recruits. At the time, Herman and I were the only Marine recruits. In my time, Marines did not draft. You enlisted.

Out of nowhere, this voice boomed, "All right, you feather merchants, line up over here." I'll never forget the look on Herman's face. He turned to me and said, "What in the hell did you get me into?" We got on a bus and headed for the Marine Corps Depot for basic training.

The first order of business was a trip to the Barber. They shaved all of my hair. Then, we were fitted for Greens – which at that time, was the dress attire. We were also fitted for fatigues, shoes, socks, underwear, rifles, toiletries, pith helmet, made out of cardboard with the Marine Corps Emblem made out of metal and a cunt cap.

Been in a Military Training camp, I felt right at home. Herman had the bottom bunk and I had the top. My first meal in the Chow Hall was dinner. It was great. You could have all the food you wanted. The next morning, at 5:00 a.m., a bugle sounding revelry awakened me. I had 5 minutes to make my bed, get dressed and meet outside the bungalow for roll call. Then the platoon Sgt. entered the barracks and inspected every bed. He drops a dime on the blanket. If it doesn't bounce you have to remake it until it does. Needless to say, mine always bounced.

I sent a portion of my military pay to my mother in Douglas to help with her expenses. I also was insured for $10,000 in the event I was killed in combat.

The training that I received at Fort Huachuca enabled me to make PFC within two weeks. I assisted the drill instructors in training my own platoon in close order drills. I made marksman with my rifle at the firing range during basic.

One day, during a rest period in our bungalow, Herman and I entertained our platoon with the song, "Alla En El Rancho

Grande". All of a sudden, the drill instructor busted open the barracks door and yelled at the top of his lungs, "Who in the hell's making this racket?"

No one said a word.

With that, the Drill Sgt. said he was going to punish the entire platoon unless someone spoke up. Herman and I stepped forward and admitted to singing. Our punishment was to get two empty steel buckets each, march to the sand dunes, one hundred yards away, fill the buckets with sand, take them back to our bungalow and empty them on the ground. We did this twice. Then, we had to fill the buckets with the sand at our bungalow and return it to the sand dunes. We were then ordered to retrieve our rifles and come outside. When we walked in the bungalow, our platoon was quiet. We had to take a hold of our 8-pound rifle and hold it in front of our bodies with arms extended. We then had to lift it straight up and then lower it behind our heads 100 times without stopping. Needless to say, we didn't sing again.

Herman was furious. I remember he looked at me and said, "Do not talk to me, in fact, I don't want you to even look at me. I don't want anyone to think we know each other."

He eventually calmed down, but boy did it take a while.

Joe E. Carlson,
Mentor
Superintendent

My Father Alex
Lou McKay

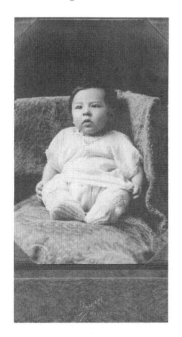

My Baby Picture
when I was a few
months old. Named
after my Mom and
Dad. Alex and Luisa
Mckay

CHAPTER 8 Accepted To The Elite Carson Raiders

At the end of boot camp, Herman and I were transferred to the Carson Raider Battalion at Camp Onofre – located on the North side of Camp Pendleton.

A Raider is an elite marine that destroys communication before the marine infantry division lands on the beach and attacks.

The survival rate is less than ten percent.

The training is mentally and physically rigorous. A knife is the only weapon you have. A Raider attack takes place at night. The enemy guards and communication sites were the target. By the end of training, I had to be able to survive in hand-to-hand combat using my knife with both the left and right hand. The training consisted of running up and down the Onofre Mountains for physical endurance and conditioning. We would have practice drills in the mountains where dummies were placed in obscure places. We would have to throw the knife until we hit our target in the throat. The advantage of having a knife as a weapon is that it's a silent killer. The drills and conditioning would take place the first part of the day and the obstacle course would take up the rest of the day — sometimes the training would last 24 hours and sleep was prohibited.

It was my job to stay awake any way I could. For me, the hours between 2:00 a.m. and 4:00 a.m. were the hardest. I remember singing songs that I learned in Douglas as a child to myself in order to stay awake and keep my mind alert.

One training exercise stands out in my memory. I had to jump off a platform, the height of a ship, jump off into the ocean, with legs crossed and hands cupped over my privates. You had to know how to jump off and swim in the event that your ship was torpedoed and you had to abandon ship.

We were granted liberty every two weeks. The list of our Raiders was divided into 2 groups: A-M and N-Z. This way, there was always a Marine on duty. When my name was called, I would head to the Paymaster at the Battalion Headquarters and pickup my $25 cash for the weekend. San Diego was a Navy town, so Herman and I would hitchhike up to Los Angeles.

In amidst of a lot of papers, I pick up a letter addressed to my mother. The return address reads: Cissy Saperstein. Boy does this bring back a memory. I met Cissy on one of my liberties. She worked as a clerk at a jewelry store adjacent to the entrance of the Roosevelt Hotel. One day, I walked in to browse and she took my breath away. She had such beautiful brunette hair, a nice shape and an infectious smile. We started to talk and seemed to hit it off right away. It was like love at first sight. Heck, I wanted to marry her right then and there. But, before I wore out my welcome, I told her I would see her again in two weeks. I left and joined the rest of the marines downstairs in the bar. I couldn't stop thinking about her. I was already looking forward the next time I would see her.

We met up again and this time Cissy wanted to introduce me to her girlfriends. We all got along great. Each time I would go up to LA, I would drop by the jewelry store and wait for her to get off work and then we would go out on a date. She liked the fact that I didn't join the other marines down in the bar or smoke with the rest of them. Being around Cissy was a breath of fresh air from the mental conditioning of the Raider Training.

When I returned back to the Raiders, I had to be able to switch gears. You had to reprogram yourself to listen to orders given and not what your body needed or cried out for. This mindset is designed to help you survive in any kind of combat, to realize that you are no longer a civilian, but a trained killer.

Raider Training helped fine-tune my survival mode. The Japanese are trained as children to become warriors and to kill for their country and emperor. In order to survive as a marine, I had to have their mindset. Kill or be killed. By the end of the training, Herman and I were able to throw our knives accurately and hit the throat every time.

When the Raiders were disbanded, Herman and I were transferred to Camp Pendleton, in Oceanside, California. Herman was assigned to the 105-millimeter artillery and I was assigned to the 75 millimeters — all part of the Artillery Battery, 10th Marines, Howitzer Battalion, and 2nd Marine Division.https://www.**youtube**.com/watch?v=WwOFTAzW30E

Cissy Saperstein   **Louis A. Mckay**

In order to understand our training to be a Carlson Raider, this classic Hollywood war movie is based on the true-life World War II

Makin Islands raid by Lieutenant Colonel Evans Carlson's 2nd Marine Raider Battalion (17–18, August 1942). It was an attack on Japanese forces on Makin (now known as Butaritari) in the Pacific Ocean.The mission was to destroy Japanese installations, take prisoners, gather intelligence on the Gilbert Islands and divert Japanese attention from Allied landings on Guadalcanal and Tulagi. An all star cast includes Randolph

Scott, Robert Mitchum, J. Carol Naish, Rod Cameron and Noah Beery Jr., is narrated by NBC News legend Chet Huntley. This film is now public domain. This movie was shot near Camp Onofre, close to Camp Pendleton, and I was an extra going through training. GUNG HO! Taken to mean 'work together' and adopted as a slogan by US Marines.

Within a few months, my division of 2500 Marines was scheduled to depart to the Hawaiian Islands for amphibious training.

My relationship with Cissy at this point was serious.

Upon winning $125 at a poker game, I decided to ask her to marry me on my next trip to LA.

I remember this day, like it was yesterday. When I arrived at the jewelry store, I walked in and stood by the door. Before I could get a word out, she walked up, gave me a kiss, and put a Silver ID bracelet on my wrist. The Marine emblem was engraved on the top and on the backside was my name and serial number. I grinned and said, "Pick out your engagement ring, I have $125 to spend."

___The Marine emblem was engraved on the top and on the backside was my name and serial number. I grinned and said, "Pick out your engagement ring, I have $125 to spend."

Within minutes, we were engaged. We went out for a nice dinner and celebrated. I was the happiest I've ever been. There was nothing sexual about our relationship. Cissy and I wanted to share our first  time together after we got married. She wanted to have my mother's address in Douglas, so they could correspond while I was overseas.

During my last liberty, I met Cissy's parents. Her father was cordial but that's it. Cissy nor I said a word about our engagement gifts. When it was time for me to return back to Camp Pendleton, Cissy held me close and said, "Please come back safe. I love you."

My Gift to mom in Uniform and framed under glass

*Cissy and me on a date, before going
overseas.*

CHAPTER 9 Second Marine Division Boards Troopship

The day we boarded our troop ship, the Second Marine Division headed for the Hawaiian Islands. The Red Cross nurses handed out cartons of Lucky Strikes cigarettes to every marine as they boarded the troop ship. I didn't smoke, but I took a carton anyway. Heck, I could sell it and make some money.

At first, it was great being on a ship for the first time. I was really looking forward to my first combat. However, when our ship entered a powerful storm, I was never so seasick in my life. Even the seasoned sailors or old salts were heaving their guts out. When I would start to feel better, I would glance up and see someone vomiting and it would start all over again.

Once we reached Oahu, we set up camp. It was then that I learned that we were the replacements for the casualties of Iwo Jima and that the armed forces of the United States had repelled the Japanese in their attempt to attack the United States by way of the Aleutian Islands, near Alaska. The Japanese had filled helium balloons headed for the islands with explosives. But they were not successful. The media never discussed this.

Our landing training consisted of loading onto the Amtracs in an assimilation attack on an island.

In the beginning, I noticed that replacements, like me, were never included in poker games, activities or even conversations with the seasoned (battled hardened) marines — the survivors of Iwo Jima.

One day, I went up to a seasoned marine and asked, "What the hell is going on here. Aren't we all Marines? We're all wearing the same uniform."

He answered with a scowl, "You're not a Marine until you've been tested. We don't know if you are going to run, fight, or die, and neither do you."

That was enough for me. At least I knew where I stood.

The 2nd Marine Division had a mascot — a duck named Siwasha. Boy did he love beer. I remember laughing with Herman and seeing this duck go from tent-to-tent sipping beer from the marines. Needless to say, by the time he reached the last tent in the row, he was wobbling back and forth, unable to sustain his balance. I never knew what happened to Siwasha. We had to leave him behind when we went into battle.

I received letters from Cissy at least once or twice a week. I was on cloud nine when I heard my name called for mail. She would tell me how much she missed me and how much she loved me. It was her letters that kept up my morale. The military always made sure that mail was delivered, regardless of our location.

Once our division was at full strength and well trained, we embarked to the Mariana Islands. Our first attack was the Island of Saipan. We waited on the LST (Landing Ship Transporter) for the 2nd Marine Infantry Division to secure the beachhead of the Japanese held Island of Saipan.

Once the infantry disembarked onto the beach, I witnessed the wounded on Amtracs headed to the hospital ship.

When I saw the bloody and bandaged, I thought, "What the hell did you get yourself into?"

My raider training snapped me back into the task at hand. I could not become emotionally involved with the wounded. So much devastation reinforced what I was there to do.

Once orders were given for the battery artillery to load, we headed down to the bottom of the ship and loaded onto the Amtracs. Our mission was to support the Marines as they continued their advancement from the beach. We filled the boats, headed out and circled the ship until we were all in line and ready to head for the beach.

While we were in route, Japanese "Kamikaze" attacked our ships from the air. This was their combat strategy; if they destroyed our ships, we would have no place to retreat. Gunfire was everywhere. As I approached shore, dead marines littered the beach. Shell holes at the water's edge were filled with bodies torn apart — blood splattered everywhere. The bloody color and smell of death is something that I'll never forget.

Once the ramp of the Amtrac was lowered, all of us pushed the 75 mm artillery onto the beach. We loaded and open fired on the Japs. By doing so, the existing marines on the beach were able to advance and to change from a defensive position to an offensive position. We all were of the same mindset — to annihilate the enemy. It was at this point, that I became a battle-hardened marine. The Japanese was trying to force us back to the ocean with everything they had and prevent us from advancing over the embankment of the island. Their attack failed. We made it, and headed inland. The Japanese ran toward us screaming "Bonsai" in a suicidal attack. Marines were dropping like flies all around me, but so were the Japanese. I felt determined in amidst the hailstorm of gunfire to keep moving forward and not wither into immobility.

The Japanese had constructed coconut pillboxes or blockhouses reinforced with steel. These barricades were virtually indestructible against gunfire or bombing. When our gunfire proved ineffective in destroying the log bunkers, flamethrowers were called in to destroy them. And they did. This allowed us to advance onto our next target. We fought tirelessly for days in support of our infantry. One day, at dawn, was suddenly awakened by suicidal "Bonsai" attacks. We soon learned that the Japanese had broken through the Army lines and was heading toward our Marine lines. We lowered our artillery muzzle to a waistline height and open fired.

We turned our muzzles toward the screaming and oncoming Japs and fired until the advancing hoard was eliminated. As a loader, I focused on the task at hand and loaded the artillery shells as fast we fired. I loaded so fast that it reached a point that the muzzles to the artillery guns were too hot to touch.

In the midst of the gunfire, I realized that I couldn't hear anything. I forgot to put in my earplugs during the dawn attack. As a result, I lost my hearing for three days.

Once the island of Saipan was secure by the 2nd Marine Division, we set up camp to replenish the casualties, wounded, and re-train the new recruits. I soon realized that my battery treated the new recruits the same way they treated all of us were baptized in combat.

There are many pictures of me in uniform. I was very proud to be a Marine and still am. Pictures of my Marine buddies are in envelopes. Our losses were heavy but we prevailed.

One afternoon, I observed a group of Marines going back to the battleground. They were the burial detail, and had the gruesome task of going in and gathering dog tags off of the bodies and body parts. The dog tag signifies name, serial number, rank and branch of service. When a body or body part is found without a tag, they are classified as "The Unknown Soldier." A bulldozer comes in and digs a trench. The detail then positions each body side by side. Afterwards, a Chaplin comes and gives the last rites before the dirt-filled bulldozer covers and

seals the burial site. White crosses are then erected above each Marine with their name, rank and the letters, USMC.

When the island was secured and in the hands of the United States Marines, I went to look for Herman. He was a loader for the 105-millimeter artillery. I stopped a passing jeep and asked if he knew where the 105s were located on the island. I jumped in and he took me right to the location.

As soon as I saw Herman, I yelled, "Hey, Muscles."

Herman turned around and smiled, "I'm glad you made it."

During our lunch of sea rations, we both talked about how damn grateful we were to be alive. Herman was training to go to Guam. After our lunch, we said our goodbyes and I returned back to camp.

We were waiting for the new recruits to arrive from Hawaii and continue training the recruits already there, our mind and bodies were exhausted from the battles.

Physical activity as well as relaxation was vital during this rebuilding mode.

Letters from my Cissy and my mother kept me going. When someone didn't receive any mail, a bunch of us would read each other's letter a loud.

It was even worse when one of our buddies received a 'Dear John' letter. I remember standing in line one day for chow, and all of sudden, we heard a rifle shot. We all hit the ground. I later learned that he had received a letter from his loved one saying that she had found someone else in the states.

It took awhile to get over that one. He was a nice guy.

When things settled down, baseball games resumed at the makeshift baseball field. This one particular day, the catcher was having difficulty because the pitcher kept throwing knuckle balls. It's a wobbly thrown ball that is difficult for the batter to hit and the catcher to catch. Consequently, once the batter reaches first base, he's almost guaranteed to steal second base when the catcher drops the ball. When the catcher drops the ball, the runner would steal third base. After a few times, I asked the coach if I could give it a try and see if I could catch the knuckle balls. I did just fine, and there was no more base stealing.

Within days, we were given orders to board a troop ship and head to our next target. While on ship, we were told we were headed to Tinian. Their airfield could accommodate our heavy B-29 Bombers.

The 2nd Marine Division's first task was to secure the airfield (annihilate the enemy resistance) so that our fighters and big bombers could land. After a desperate attempt by the Japanese on Tinian, at 2 a.m., they tried to push us out to sea. We stopped their attack and killed every one of them. We shot so many at a time that they began to pile up on each other's bodies. I am 5'8" and I couldn't see over them. I was possessed with so much adrenaline and hate that after it was over, I didn't even notice that the marine on my left and on my right had been killed.

My battery returned back to Saipan to regroup and replenish the thousands of casualties we endured. Without fail, a letter from Cissy would be waiting for me. When we were ready to proceed onto to our next unknown target, I learned that an officer of the day, found one of our guards asleep on duty 3 days before we were to go into battle.

A guard's job is to make sure that no enemy infiltrates and that the resting marines are protected at all times. Every marine is assigned even if you have combat fatigue. When an officer finds a guard asleep on his watch, his rifle is removed and he is awakened and replaced. When the rifle is confiscated, the guard can't say he wasn't asleep. He's immediately sent to the brig (jail) and fed only bread and water.

The guard's job during combat is a (Forward Observer). His job is to direct the artillery shots for our battery. When it was my turn to guard, I was determined to stay awake. I sang silently from the Hit Parade magazine, like "At Last," "Show Me The Way Home," "Once In A While"and "Hey Good Lookin." When I ran out of English songs, I would sing "Cielito Lindo," "Guadalajara," and of course, Herman's and my favorite, "Alla en el Rancho Grande."

Now that our guard was in the brig, our battery was without a forward observer. I volunteered to take his place, so I could be with the infantry — the area between the artillery and the enemy.

Armed only with a carbine and headphones, I now had the responsibility to learn how to give the correct elevation and latitude of the 75-millimeter artillery to the gunners of the battery behind me.

The goal is to destroy the enemy and not hit my own marines on the ground in front. To establish the enemy target, you give an order for a long shot, a shorter shot and the third shot. The third shot is the one that hits your target. Once the target is established, I then give an order "fire for effect." This is intended to annihilate enemy positions. In three days, the other forward observers in the Marines trained me. Upon completion, I was proficient in directing the battery. I mastered the assignment physically and mentally, so when I was in battle, I would know exactly what to do. The responsibility I had was enormous.

I respected the enemy. The Japanese are trained as children to annihilate the enemy and honor their Emperor. I was trained as a raider to be superior to any enemy. I was not there as an occupational force. This mindset is what distinguishes a marine from other armed forces. It was that confidence that enabled me to survive.

I was excited to go into battle. My 2nd Marine Division, embarked aboard ship and we were told that Okinawa was our next target. When we landed, there was little resistance. However, I had an eerie feeling that hell was about to unleash on us. It wasn't until our division traveled south to the outskirts of Naha did hell Un-leash its fury. We encountered heavy resistance from what seemed to be thousands of Japanese coming at us from all directions. Armed with my phone and a small rifle (carbine) — in charge of four 75 millimeters, my infantry advanced in the attack mode.

Along with thousands of fellow marines, my platoon entered with approximately 180 men. We ran fast charging toward the enemy. When shells hit the ground, they made huge shell holes, lifting and exploding the ground around us.

We ran up the mountainside and down into the rice paddy, dodging the artillery and then we proceeded up the side of another mountain and down in the rice paddy at the bottom of another mountain. All of sudden my body flew into the air. My helmet, backpack, telephone, carbine, canteen belt, shells and bandolier were blown off. Lieutenant McCain jumped in the six-foot-sized shell hole and took off his belt and used it as a tourniquet. In my delirium, I chuckled. His pants fell to his shoes when he took off this belt. The corpsman (medic) jumped in and began to administer blood plasma, and bandaged me up to stop the flow of blood. I remember a god-awful buzzing sound in my head. I reached over and noticed a Dandelion. I grabbed it and remembered saying, "You got to live, you son of a bitch." I kept it in my hand until I was put on a truck and transferred to a piper cub (small plane with baskets on each side to fly the wounded). I was then flown along with other wounded to the hospital area on the island. When I landed, medics transferred me to a cot and lined me side-by-side with the rest of the wounded.

When someone didn't make it they were taken out of line and covered with a plastic raincoat or poncho. Unfortunately, a lot of men didn't make it to the operating table. Looking back, the line seemed a block long. Men were screaming when the Morphine began to wear off. Navy medics, splattered with blood, walked up and down the isles, and snapped the big toes of the wounded. If you didn't respond, chances were you're not going to make it.

I remember having feeling in my left leg. I must have dozed off because the next thing I remember is waking up in the hospital tent. I turned my head and a fellow marine lay beside me looking at a picture. He said, "This is my wife and my two little girls. The corpsman that jumped in after you was killed right after they pulled you out. Boy, you are lucky to be alive. My Lt., said the Japs are masters of camouflage. Those mountains that we ran up and over had rotating artilleries with metal tracks built inside the lava-mountains, that made it easy for them to fire in 4 different directions. I didn't even see them. Those sons of bitches just let us run right over them and then once we were in the rice paddy down below, they open fired."

A nurse came in and gave me a shot and I must have blacked out. When I came to, the pain was excruciating. The cot next to me was gone. I asked the medic where my buddy was. He said he didn't make it. The guy had a wife and two little girls waiting at home for him. I thought to myself, "Why him and not me?"

I recall lying on a bunk on the hospital ship, Solace. A doctor came to my ward and said, "Your entire left side has suffered extensive damage from the shrapnel of the artillery shell. Your left leg is so mangled, that your better off without it." I sat up and looked him dead in the eyes, "If you cut it off, without my permission, I'll find you, and I'll kill you."

When the United States secured the island of Okinawa, the hospital ship Solace loaded the last of the casualties and sailed to San Francisco Military Hospital - a receiving hospital where the wounded are flown to a military hospital nearest to their home. I chose San Diego Naval Hospital. It was close to my hometown of Douglas and to Cissy in Los Angeles.

The objective of this military operation was to seize the islands closest to Japan. After our long campaign of island hopping, Okinawa served as a springboard for the planned invasion of the islands. With the atomic bombings on Hiroshima and Nagasaki Japan and the threat of another on Tokyo, Japan surrendered.

General Douglas MacArthur witnesses Japan's Surrender 1945

CHAPTER 10 – My Family Visits At The San Diego Naval Hospital

The hospital ward was filled with wounded men. Pacific Bell had arranged to have a telephone jack installed at each bedside. Each of us was given a free 30-minute phone call.

My first call was to Cissy so I could tell her where I was... .Then, I called my mother. When she heard my voice, she sobbed. She told me that a young man, by the name Medigovich, a fellow marine in Okinawa, called her and said that I had been so severely wounded that he didn't know whether I had survived.

Within a short time, my family from Douglas surprised me with a visit. I remember when my mother came to my bedside. She broke down and sobbed. It hurt to talk because the Shrapnel had damaged my mouth.

While I was in the hospital and even today, people have a hard time grasping why I am not bitter or angry with what happened to me.

I became a Marine on my volition. No one forced me. In war, I did my job and the Japanese did theirs. This mindset helped me cope with adversities of being in danger of losing my life. My injuries were a casualty of war. My only regret is that I wasn't able to finish the job.

I would read in the newspaper and hear on the radio, the important role women played while our country was at war. When the United States entered the Second World War, "Rosie the Riveter" became the symbol for women workers in the American defense industries. The diversion of men from the labor pool into the military, as well as the increased production, needed to support the war effort prompted the federal War Manpower Commission.The Office of War Information undertook a nationwide campaign to recruit women into the labor force.

During the war years, women became taxicab drivers, business managers, commercial airline checkers, aerodynamic engineers, and railroad workers. They operated machinery, streetcars, buses, cranes, and tractors. They unloaded freight, worked in lumber mills and steel mills, and made munitions, sewed military apparel, made gas masks, parachutes, helmets, bullets, jeeps, tanks, prepared and packed sea rations for the military.

The women built ships and airplanes next to men that did not qualify to serve in the military. They served as ferry and test pilots, mechanics, flight controllers, instructors, and aircraft production line workers. If you were 18 years of age or older, you were eligible to participate in the war effort. It was mandated by congress and signed by the Commander-in-Chief.

At the Hollywood Canteen and the USO (United States Organization) ladies also played a key role helping to raise the morale of our troops by attending dances and military functions.

The women helped support their families while their men were fighting for our country. When the service men returned, they had to find other work, because the women did not want to relinquish their jobs or their wages, like they did after World War I. This newfound freedom for women across the country enabled them, for the first time, to become financially independent. Women now occupied every aspect of industry during the war.

I am amazed that I had a smile on my face in most of my pictures, as I sifted through pictures of me while I was at the San Diego Naval Hospital. My nurses', corpsmen and doctors were at my bedside and my left leg was raised in a sling and bandages covered my entire left side.

Cissy visited me almost every weekend. Hell, I hardly had any teeth left, and I remember being uncomfortable.

The naval hospital had different buildings for the military wounded. I was located in Building 10, 3rd floor. This hospital housed the wounded from the Navy and the Marines.

Since my wounds covered such a large area, the procedures to remove the shrapnel took a long time. I had to wait my turn for the operating room. The doctors had to address the most grave of injuries in order to prevent infection.

The doctors proceeded to operate and remove bone from my right leg shinbone and then graph that over to my mangled left leg. I endured skin and bone graphs every 3 weeks for 2 years. I needed new teeth on my left side because a piece of shrapnel had pierced my jaw. Since my wounds covered my entire left side; it was difficult for the pain medication to cover every area that was in need of relief.

Visits from Cissy made it easier. She tried to comfort me in my recovery, but it was difficult.

The type of skin graph used on me, commonly called 'the sausage' is made up of rolled up flesh from a healthy part of the body. Doctors must use flesh instead of skin. It contains corpuscles that are vital in helping keep the flesh alive. Because the area between my knee and left ankle were held together by the calf muscle and skin, 14 inches in diameter of flesh, from my abdominal area were cut and rolled into the shape of a sausage.

After three week's time, they cut the end of the sausage and attached it to my left forearm. I stayed twisted in a sideways position for three weeks. Once that portion was successful, the doctor's removed the other portion of the sausage that was attached to my tummy area and attached that to my left forearm. I was finally able to lie on my back. Unfortunately, not without pain as shrapnel had entered my left side and I had to stay in that position for another three weeks.

When that was a success, the doctors were now ready for the bone graphs. Shrapnel had blown the area between my knee and ankle away. The doctors used part of my right shin for the bone graph in an effort to enforce the left leg. After the bone graphs had taken and deemed a success, the doctors removed the sausage from my left forearm, unrolled it and applied it to the entire front portion of my left shin area. This one operation took nine hours and would take a minimum of six weeks for recovery.

Since I had endured so many operations already, my heart strength began to falter. I was later told that they almost lost me on the operating table.

The skin graphs had to take in order for the operation to be a success, with it, my hand and arm would finally be free.

I began to be concerned because Cissy's visits became less frequent. I managed to reach one of her girlfriends and she got in touch with Cissy.

To this day, I don't remember how I managed to travel up to Los Angeles to see her, but I did. When we met, she started to cry. Cissy told me that her father would never approve of our relationship. Since her family was Jewish and I was, Catholic. She told me that she could never go against the wishes of her parents. With that, she put the ring in the palm of my hand and told me that she could never see me again. We hugged each other and cried for a long time. Finally, she broke away and left. I held on to her ring for quite awhile. Several liberties later, I traveled to the Santa Monica Pier and threw the ring into the ocean.

I took time out everyday at the Naval Hospital to pray in the chapel. I pleaded for God to save my leg.

One evening, after visiting hours, I looked up and saw Herman walking towards my bed. Boy was he a welcomed sight. I was in so much pain, for so long that I was glad to see someone else besides the staff. We were so glad to see each other. My bed was right by a window, so I threw out the water in the plastic pitcher and handed it to Herman.

He pulled out a bottle of Jack Daniels from the inside of his coat and filled the pitcher. Needless to say, we both got plastered. We laughed so loud, that everyone around us must have known what we were up to. Nobody said a word or complained of the noise, not even the nurses on the night shift.

On another occasion, a mother, who lost one of her twin boys in the South Pacific, would come by and bring fruit to all the wounded men in the ward. She knitted me a quilt with my name on it. I still have it to this day.

One afternoon after the nurses made their rounds, I called Mr. Carlson. He too had heard that I was severely wounded and was glad to hear my voice. We chatted a long time on the phone and promised to continue to stay in touch.

The doctors were now ready to remove the bandages. Unfortunately, the skin graph did not adhere and came off leaving my bone graph exposed once again. Gangrene had started to travel up the leg, and doctors were concerned that I could also lose my knee. Maggots were applied so they could eat up all the pus and infection. It didn't matter how much pain medication they would administer, and it was never enough.

The infection was traveling so fast my bone started to turn brown. I called my doctor. He suggested we take one of my rib bones to help rebuild my left shin.

I asked him, "After you do all of this, and let's say it's a success, will I be able to walk and have full use of my leg?"

I'll never forget his response, "You will drag it for the rest of your life."

After he left, I called Dr. Capt. Wire, head of the Orthopedic Department and asked him to come and see me. I asked, "How soon can we take this damn thing off?" He answered, "How about first thing tomorrow morning? We'll remove your leg four inches below your knee." I said, "Fine."

Part of me was very disappointed, because my prayers were not answered. However, to still be alive, was a victory.

The hospital had two years to save my leg, and put me back together. How was I going to make a living for myself? How was I going to manage with a wooden leg? In my mind, I was a cripple. I finally had to accept that saving my leg was not going to happen. The next morning, I was awakened by the Corpsman. He wheeled me into a very cold operating room. The doctor, then gave me a saddle block so I wouldn't feel anything. Several times, I had to reassure the nurses that I didn't feel anything. They talked to me throughout the procedure and tried to distract me from what the doctor was doing. I felt a sense of relief knowing that I had made the right choice to save my knee. All of a sudden, I heard part of my leg fall into the bucket. Even though I didn't feel anything, I was wide-awake and aware. When I returned to my ward and settled in, I rose up to see my left limb to see if I had been dreaming.

The doctors had to stretch the skin enough to cover the four-inch stump, and then tape the skin on my thigh and knee. They then stretched it over the open stump with two twenty-pound metal weights. I could still feel my missing limb. Your brain still monitors signals throughout your entire body, even with the loss of a limb. When the saddle block began to wore off, the nurse was right there with pain medication. All of a sudden, I had an involuntary reflex and yanked the weights up into my bed, barely missing my right leg. To avoid further injury, the doctors went ahead and sewed the stump shut. I had become accustomed to pain having had so many surgeries throughout my lengthy hospital stay that removing my limb seemed like a blessing.

One afternoon, a nurse who had followed my rehabilitation over the last years, mentioned that my chart indicated I had received over 90,000 units of Penicillin. As I sifted through more pictures, I came across one with Sgt. Tony Diaz, my marine buddy in Japan, and four marine buddies. I just sit and stared. Out of 180 men in my platoon, I was one of the six survivors. I'm damn lucky to be alive!

*The Nurses at the Hospital were outstanding and helped me
with my recovery*

CHAPTER 11 – Recovery From My Leg Amputation

Once I recovered from the amputation, I was eager to get on with my life. Nobody in the hospital seemed to know what my steps were going to be in regarding to my rehabilitation. This lasted for quite a long time and it frustrated me.

Mr. Carlson phoned me to check on my progress. I shared my frustration with him how slow things were moving along. The next morning, the head surgeon for the ward stopped by my bed.

He said, "I don't know who this Joe E. Carlson is from Douglas, but evidently he called in and complained that we weren't moving fast enough to help your progress of your rehabilitation."

Within days, I was flown to Mare Island Naval Hospital, in Vallejo, California to begin my rehabilitation. At the time, San Diego didn't have a prosthetics' facility.

Since my legs were immobile for over 2 years, atrophy had set in. I had to exercise my left leg rigorously with leather and steel pulleys in order to build my strength and muscles. The pain was excruciating. I had to start learning to stand and walk with my new leg. It was an arduous and painful process that took a lot of time and practice. It took months before I was able to walk on my own without the aid of crutches or a cane.

I didn't know how to cope with the loss of my leg. As a marine in combat, my purpose was fulfilled – I avenged my schoolmates who lost their lives in New Guinea. Now I wanted to be a part of something, but what? I didn't know what I was going to do for a career. I had to make a living. My compensation from the military for wounds suffered was not going to be enough to make ends meet. Part of me felt inadequate, half of a man, a cripple. I told my mom I was incomplete and she said, "NO, that is not so."

The mindset I had as a young boy when faced with adversities instilled the strength in me to cope with any situation. My limitations were physical not mental. My leg didn't take away who I was as person, and it certainly wasn't going to take my pride and run it into the ground. The best thing I could do for myself is to get on with my life and make the best of it.

I called my family and Joe E. Carlson to tell them that I was now in Vallejo.

When it came time to custom make my prosthetic leg, the military sent me by Jitney Cab (a golf cart like vehicle) from Vallejo to San Francisco.

Carl Woodall, the inventor of the artificial limb was located in San Francisco. He worked extensively with the wounded servicemen.

In 1947, prosthetics was made of wood. In order for the stump to fit correctly into the artificial cup, both Carl and his foreman, Neil, made a plaster cast of my limb. They matched the height of the right leg so that my gate and hips would remain balanced. They even made a foot the same shoe size as mine so I could purchase shoes. A wide, thick leather belt had to be worn to keep the artificial leg attached to the stump. In addition, a metal hook was attached to the thick leather shoelaces of the leather thigh holster. To keep the leg in place, the sides were reinforced with iron brackets. There were numerous fittings, cuttings, plaster moldings, and adjustments before my prosthesis fit properly. Precise alignment is crucial so it would be like walking with my own leg. It took four months before my prosthetic leg was complete.

I needed a break from the hospital routine and asked for liberty. I took the Jitney to downtown Vallejo to have a bite of real food and a drink of rum and Coca Cola. On crutches, I maneuvered my way into a little restaurant. It was there that I met Doris (my first wife). She was a waitress. When business was slow, Doris would sit down and visit with her customers.

We hit it off. She was pretty, had a nice shape and beautiful auburn hair. Doris had a little girl named Beverly, who lived with her grandparents in Vallejo, while she worked evenings and attended beauty school during the day.

Over the next few months I spent my liberties visiting Doris, her parents and getting to know Beverly. Doris soon graduated from beauty school, passed the state board and received her license to be a hairdresser.

One day at lunch, Doris sat down and told me that her mother mentioned that she could have Beverly live with her once she got married. I remember looking at Doris and I said, "Well, let's get married."

So, on my next liberty, I borrowed some money from my friends and we took off on a bus to Reno and got married. When we returned, Doris found us a place at Mare Island Naval

Housing. Since I was still in rehabilitation, I would take the

Jitney to and from our apartment.

Married life seemed good and we all got along great. Doris

had a job at a beauty shop and I received an increase in my

subsistence now that I was married and had a child to support.

Beverly was such a sweet little girl, very loving especially to

me. She would call me 'daddy'.

I came across my military discharge papers , July 15,

1947,Vallejo, California.

One day, there was a knock at the door, Mare Island Hospital

notified me by telegram stating that Adolfo Cruz had passed

away. I immediately contacted my mother in Douglas.

As soon as she said, "I need you," I requested a fifteen day

leave of absence from the Marine Corps.

Once Doris heard of the news, she was very supportive in

my decision to go back and help my mother and the family.

With Beverly in school during the day, Doris was able to go to

work and not have to worry about childcare.

My commanding officer suggested an immediate honorable

discharge, that way, the Military would pay for my flight and I

could stay as long as I was needed and still receive my

severance check. With discharge papers in hand, I remember leaving the hospital feeling a sense of relief, but on the other hand, I was apprehensive. I didn't know what my life had in store for me. With my country still at war, I was going to do whatever I had to do to make a living for my family and myself.

When I arrived in Douglas, Adolfo's family had arranged to have my mother and all the siblings driven to Williams to bury Adolfo in his family plot. Since my mother had received a life insurance policy from the Smelter, Adolfo's family wanted my mother to pay for her portion of the funeral expenses once she arrived. I told them, "Absolutely not! She has three children to care for."

Although his life insurance policy would help support the family for a time and defray some expenses, she was still a widow with three small children under the age of 10.
After Adolfo's burial, we all boarded a train and headed back to Douglas.

Once everything settled, I needed to get back to Vallejo. The day I was scheduled to leave, I sat my mother down and told her that I was out of the military and she would no longer receive her allotment. She was very surprised to hear of my discharge but not as much as she was when she heard that I was now married and had a family to support.

My mother was livid. She thought that I had been drugged to make such a rash decision without including her or even notifying her. She thought I lost my mind.

I wanted to drop by 15th Street Baseball Field and see if anyone was playing. To my surprise, a group of my baseball buddies were practicing. I remember when they saw me like it was yesterday. They ran up and asked me how I was doing. They heard that I had lost my leg and was seriously wounded. They didn't know if I survived.

Amado Gutierrez (aka Chief), the pitcher, asked, "You wanna a hit a ball?"

Of course, I said, "Yes."

I smiled and picked up the bat. I remember I swung with all the strength I had. Unfortunately, I missed, and the prosthesis detached itself and I fell to the ground. Everyone came running to help me. I started to laugh. The guys seemed to be relieved that took what just happened in such good spirits.

This was the beginning of accepting my disability.

CHAPTER 12 Transition From Military Life To Civilian

When I returned to Vallejo, the level of combat stress made the transition from military life to civilian life extremely difficult. Not only did I endure years rehabilitating my body, but also I now had to condition my mind to conform to the ways of civilian life. As a marine in combat, I had to be in survival mode at all times. Apart from the moral deformity resulting from the sudden release of adrenaline, there were two fundamental experiences that threatened to damage my character as a liberated marine.

When I returned to civilian life, I was disillusioned with the attitude of many civilians. I was met with a shrug of a shoulder, and phrases, such as:

"We didn't know about it?"

"We too have suffered!"

"We had to ration food and gas!"

"We tucked in our belts, so that we could help you win the war!"

I felt like crawling in a hole and not seeing another human being!

Individuals who worked in the factories to supply war materials to the service people have my greatest admiration. Civilians who did not work towards the war effort sacrificed on their own behalf. In my eyes fate was cruel. By losing half my left limb by an artillery shell, I thought I had endured and reached the absolute limit of suffering, only to find that suffering has no limits, and that I will likely continue to suffer. The only difference now is my mindset.

When I returned to Vallejo, Doris was upset that her parents had moved to San Francisco. So I offered to move so she could be close to her parents.

I contacted the VA in San Francisco and they recommended Diamond Cutting. In this trade, you're responsible for cutting the correct raw diamond and making it into specific sizes and cuts. One single mistake on my part and it would cost the company thousands of dollars. That was not the trade for me. I went back to the VA and they suggested watch-making. Day in and day out, you work with tiny components on the inside of a watch. This trade required a great deal of patience and I didn't have it. So, I returned back to the VA. This time, they suggested I train to be a silversmith. In this trade, you start out with crude silver and then make it into hollow ware and flatware. The majority of the job consisted of the machine doing the work. I was only in the trade a short time when I found out that the most I could make in a week was $75. I was a silversmith long enough to make a sterling silver chain and locket for my mother.

One evening, I remember talking to Doris about how frustrated I was, and that I wanted to get into a specialty trade where I could make some good money and create something. Doris suggested beauty school.

It was 1948, when men were just beginning to enter the cosmetology field. I told her that I would consider it but not in San Francisco. Doris's mother had strong influence on her and it was unsettling. It seemed that wherever her mother moved, Doris wanted to be near her. Granted, her mother did take good care of Beverly. However, I felt that if I moved Doris away she could stand on her own two feet.

Herman and I kept in contact after he left the Marines for civilian life. He lived in Eagle Rock, a suburb of Los Angeles. He was now married and working for the Gas Company.

We moved to Los Angeles, California and Beverly stayed behind to live with her grandparents while Doris and I settled in with our careers.

Consequently, I enrolled at The Empire Beauty College. While there I was shampooing hair and massaging women scalp, which was a new challenge that was definitely going to spike whatever creative juices I was about to uncover.

It was the farthest thing from a tenderhearted person. In the beginning, they trained you on styrofoam heads with wigs. I had to master the basics of hairdressing in order to work on female patrons. This was not an easy transition. For me, it was terrifying. I was very nervous about being too rough with my hands. With styrofoam you have no way to gauge your strength. The memory of my first shampoo and set still makes me laugh.

The look on the lady's face while I shampooed her scalp was one of terror. She looked like her eyes were about to pop out of her sockets. I towel dried and set her hair-while, concentrating on not being too rough. I combed her out, and asked her how she liked it. She looked in to my eyes and raised her voice, "Do you really want me to tell you?"

I answered, "Yes, I do." Then she said, "I have never looked, so terrible in my life!" The professor overheard the woman's comment and came up behind me and started to re-comb the patron. I thought I did a pretty good job. What did she expect for 50 cents? Perhaps I was a little rough, but the hairstyle turned out decent for my first style. Obviously, my opinion didn't matter. This experience made me more determined to improve my technique.

Within nine months, I mastered the pin curl and the finger wave. My permanent waving technique needed work. The pin curl required patience and the ability to perform tedious and repetitive maneuvers with my fingers. At times, I felt overwhelmed. Students in the beauty college would make fun of me and doubted that I would succeed after they found out I was a combat Marine. It was quite a transition from warrior to hairstylist — from a trained killer, to pampering women. Few could understand my motivation to venture into a field that was so different from where I had comeI remained focused and determined to make this my career.

Physically, my prosthesis was giving me a hard time. With every step, I had excruciating pain that just wouldn't let up. My right leg was still weak from the operations, but getting stronger every day. It was difficult to stand for any length of time, let alone put my entire weight on my good leg.

I didn't know what to do.

One day after class, I spoke with the owners of the beauty school about my painful dilemma. Thereafter, I used a rolling stool .

At night, when I would remove my prosthesis, my stump was always covered in blood. I couldn't figure out what was cutting my flesh. When I would rub my stump, I'd feel something sharp underneath the skin. I thought that this was a result of the operation. The constant pain wasn't helping calm my nerves or allow me to focus on being gentle. Finally, I couldn't bear it any longer.I went to the Memorial Hospital in Los Angeles, and requested an x-ray of my limb. I showed them where the surgeon cut off my limb, he cut it straight across and neglected to round the edges of the Fibula and Tibia. As a result, every step resulted in bone cutting through my flesh. The doctor scheduled surgery within a couple of days.

The owners of the beauty college were very understanding and told me to come back when I was able. I stayed in the hospital until my stitches were removed. My recovery was progressing nicely and the x-rays showed everything to be fine.

Toward the end of my stay, a nurse walked in and handed me a letter. I opened it up and out fell Doris's wedding ring. The letter read: "Our marriage isn't working out. I'm moving back to San Francisco to live with my parents." She didn't even sign it. I lay there and just shook my head. What was I supposed to do? Beg her to come back? Not this man! That afternoon, Herman called me and asked if I had received a letter from Doris. Evidently, she has asked him to drop by the hospital and give me my 'Dear John' letter. He refused and told her to do it herself. Herman and his wife, Jewell, offered me a room in their home once I was released from the hospital.

If the day could not have gotten any worse, another nurse walked in and handed me the daily newspaper. The United States was at war with Korea. I thought that when the United States dropped the atomic bombs on Tinian and Japan and surrendered, that would put an end to the conflict between United States and finally there would be peace. But that wasn't the case.

I felt sad that we were going to lose more American lives. The islands that I fought for were Saipan, where we lost 8000 men. On Tinian, we lost 6000 men, and on Okinawa, the United States lost 86,000 men. I continued to read articles that mention General McArthur and that he wanted to cross the 38th parallel and finish the conflict with Korea. However, President Harry Truman was not in favor of crossing, so he relieved McArthur of his command and transferred him back to the United States. To this day, I question the motivation of President Truman and his desire to continue a conflict knowing that General McArthur had the means to resolve it.

After World War II, there were millions of dollars spent on artillery and ammunition that were dumped into the ocean so that the United States could keep producing war material. When our country is in conflict, our economy thrives. It always has and always will. Congress votes in favor of the money spent for war. Not one penny is allocated for peace.

As I hold a copy of my diploma from Empire Beauty College, it brings back so many memories. It was such a difficult time for me that I just wanted to get on with my life. Once I was able to put weight on my stump and navigate around, I returned to beauty school, graduated with honors and received my diploma from Empire Beauty College. The day I found out I passed my state board and was issued a California license, I was very proud of my accomplishment and myself.This was a special day for me

When I got home to Herman's place, Doris was waiting for me. She wanted me back. I remember looking around for Beverly. She left her with her parents. This bothered me. Why didn't she want her daughter around? I agreed to give our marriage another chance. Since I was living with Herman and his wife, we stayed in the spare bedroom until we found a place of our own. It wasn't very long until we found out Doris was expecting. She soon found a job working in a beauty salon as a beautician and I scouted the area for salons that specialized in the permanent wave.

My ambition was to be the best, but more importantly, I needed to make a living and survive. So I inquired about beauty salons that were known for their permanent waves. I met with Mr. Milhone of the Don Milhone Salon and asked him to teach me the permanent wave technique. I was hired as his assistant. Within 3 months, I learned his technique, and applied for a job as a Hair Dresser at the Don Rito and Renard Salon in Los Angeles. Having mastered the permanent wave I also learned the art of selling and dealing with the public and their different personalities. Don Rito's motto, "Never argue or pressure the customer to spend more money then they can afford."

Even with all of my newfound talent, something was lacking. I wanted to create a hairstyle to compliment the features of each customer. Shortly, I enrolled to three days a week at Roberta Tate's Hair Styling School in Beverly Hills. She was the top hairstylist teacher in the country. It was at her school that I learned how to be an artistic hairstylist utilizing the sculpture curl and the razor cut. The sculpture curl is designed to be used on shorter lengths of the hair. The comb out is smoother because the hair is not twisted into a curl and looped into one as in the pin-curl. It has to do with how the hair is twisted around your finger to make a pin-curl. Back in the day, you were given a razor with a guard so that you wouldn't cut your fingers. Eventually, you graduated to a no-guard razor. I mastered the technique so that I didn't need a guard. The razor gave a better more unified haircut. Roberta's rule of thumb, flatter the good features of every woman. She would instruct on a specific technique on a model. She would then go around the class and make sure that the technique you were using flattered the model's features. If it didn't, she suggested other ideas.

Movie extras would often be our models for instruction. We never styled dry hair. It was always shampooed, towel-dried, and combed. While the hair is damp, combed back and then brought forward with the hands, a true hairstylist is able to determine the masculine and feminine side to a face. The damp stage acts as a road map when styling according to each client's individual features. Most of the time, the models would be pleasantly surprised because they finally had a hair style that brought out their best attributes.

There were times when women would bring in a magazine and point out a hair style that she wanted. This is where Roberta stepped in and took charge. She told them what which style would work for their features. After all, this was a school of style. The movie extras from Hollywood became my practice ground. Mrs. Tate observed my every move, and made sure all the students followed her direction and improved consistently.

I liked it when Mrs. Tate did the rounds. If I was doing something wrong, she stopped at my station. On Tuesdays,

Thursdays, and Saturdays, I would get paid to practice my new skills in a local salon in Glendale. It wasn't long before word of mouth spread about a hairstylist in Glendale, named Louis McKay. Soon, I had a following of repeat customers. I graduated and received my advanced hairstyling diploma from Roberta Tate Hairstyling School.

I was also invited to join the Hollywood Hair Design Counsel. This was an organization that judged beauty contests throughout the state of California. The counsel established such a positive reputation, that we were invited to judge an International Beauty Salon Contest at the Jack Tar Hotel in San Francisco. Representatives from France, Austria, Germany, Italy, and Britain participated in this international event. Austria won first place. I come across pictures of me in front of the Ambassador Hotel, in Los Angeles, CA. I'm posing with models looking as if I was styling their hair. In every picture, I'm dressed in a three-piece suit, hair slicked back and shoes polished.

One particular hair styling event comes to mind. The members of the Hollywood Hair Design Counsel were given a platform to showcase their artistic hairstyling talent. The hairstyle had to be unique and innovative.

I wanted flexibility so I chose a model with long hair. Within a few seconds, I had her design created in my mind. I felt a rush when I was given the freedom to create a unique hairstyle. I gave my model a 'pointed Cone' style out of the King Arthur era. The cardboard used to support the tall style was hidden with her hair from the front of the head. As a finishing touch, I sprinkled rainbow glitter over the hairstyle. As she strolled down the catwalk, the audience erupted in a loud and long applause.

As a member of the Counsel, you have to prove your worth by creating innovative hairstyles at shows, volunteering for charity, and constantly perfecting your craft. This organization of hair stylists also donated their time to help those less fortunate.

One charitable event I participated in has stayed in my memory to this day. Arrangements were made in advance for the stylists to travel by Greyhound Bus to the Rancho Los

Amigos Hospital, in Downey, California. This facility housed those suffering with Polio. Each stylist entered the facility and were immediately escorted by a nurse to their assigned patient. As I followed the nurse through the facility, there were hundreds of iron tanks that lined the walls. Every one of my patients seemed glad to see me. They already had their hair shampooed by the nurses, so all I had to do was cut their hair.

Iron-Tanks

An iron tank is a large machine that enables a person to breathe when normal muscle control has been lost or the work of breathing exceeds the person's ability. The patient is placed into the central chamber (cylindrical steel drum). A door allowing the head and neck to remain free is then closed, forming a sealed, air-tight compartment enclosing the rest of the person's body. Pumps that control airflow periodically decrease and increase the air pressure within the chamber, and particularly, on the chest. When the pressure in the lungs fall below a certain level, the lungs expand and air from the outside of the chamber is sucked in via the person's nose and airways. When the pressure rises above that within the lungs, the reverse occurs, and air is expelled. The iron lung mimics the physiologic action of breathing by periodically altering the intra thoracic pressure, causing the air to flow in and out of the lungs.

On the bus ride home, some of the stylists were visibly shaken. Perhaps it was because I spent so much time in a hospital that I was able to understand the patient's plight. I felt fortunate to have the opportunity to help someone in this state and to make them feel better even if it was for a short amount of time.

My mindset was centered on Doris and her pregnancy. She was due any day. Seeing so many people in such a dire state, I wanted to have a healthy and happy baby.

Doris McKay With New Born Bradford Douglas McKay

CHAPTER 13 My First Born Son

On June 17, 1949, Doris gave birth to my first son, Bradford Douglas McKay. I named him after my hometown of Douglas. Mr. Carlson happened to phone me. He was visiting his brother in Long Beach. I was happy to share the exciting news with him. On his way back to Douglas, he stopped by to visit me and my new son.

I was now a full-time hairstylist in Glendale. Once Doris recuperated, I couldn't figure out why she appeared nervous and unsettled. She wasn't happy and it showed in her face. One day, Doris wanted to take the Greyhound up to San Francisco and have her parents meet our new son. Once she got there, she didn't want to come home. I could never figure out the influence her parents had on her. I knew then that our marriage was going to be difficult.

In Douglas, my mother was overwhelmed with the responsibility of raising three children by herself. It was difficult to keep an eye on my family from a distance. So, I moved everyone up to Eagle Rock, got the kids settled in school, found them a little house, and my mother, a job as a cook at a local restaurant.

Needless to say, my plate was full once again. My marriage with Doris was not working out and my son was with his mother. I felt that Brad was better off with Doris and her parents..He now had someone to look after him on a consistent basis. I couldn't attend to him with my work schedule.

My mother was happy that she was close to me now. She loved her job and everyone in the family seemed to have acclimated to the new environment, except Wilford. He didn't want to leave his friends in Douglas.

Looking back, Los Angeles laid the foundation that provided the schools, salons and organizations that I needed in order to specialize in my craft — the permanent wave, haircut, hairstyling, and the comb-out. Having all of this at my disposal enabled me to succeed as a hairstylist. I would be one of many stylists if I had stayed in Los Angeles.

In 1951, there were only three known hair salons in the San Diego area - Walter's House of Beauty, Charles's Hairstyling Salon, and the Jimmie Davis House of Beauty. The first two salons were located in downtown, San Diego, on Broadway. The Jimmie Davis House of Beauty was located in Hillcrest on

Fifth and Laurel. I chose this salon because Jimmie didn't have a hairstylist.

Within three months, I was able to build my base clientele. One day, a beauty supply salesman approached me and said he had heard of my work. There was an empty salon on Fifth and Pennsylvania. Other than hair dryers and supplies, the salon was move-in ready. Later that afternoon, I looked at the salon and decided that it was perfect.

I went next door to the grocery store and inquired about the vacant salon. The owner of the store owned the salon, barber shop and the store. The rent for the salon was $80/month. The next day, I went to The Bank of America branch, downtown, and applied for a $2500 loan. My loan was approved contingent that I would agree to withdraw no more than $75 a month out of the salon until the loan was paid in full.

Soon, The Louis McKay Hair Styling Salon on 5th Avenue was in Neon Lights. The location of my salon was perfect. There was a transit stop right in front. For those who were waiting for the next bus, they would peek in and see the work in progress and admire the ladies leaving the salon. It was ideal for both marketing and advertising. My satisfied customers provided constant referrals.

Brad was now 2 years-old, and still living with his mother. I was able to send support to Brad, Doris was able to continue to work as a hairdresser in San Francisco and have her parents watch over Brad. It wasn't the ideal situation, but I was too busy trying to build my business and make a living.

I worked very hard at building a good reputation for myself, soon my reputation spread throughout the county. I looked up every Woman's Club in San Diego, La Jolla, El Cajon, La Mesa, National City, Chula Vista, Coronado, and Tijuana, Mexico.

I attended Self-Improvement classes for women held in the evenings at Roosevelt, Jr. High School. The class would teach women different ways to make themselves look and feel better about themselves. Topics covered were fashion, make-up, and hair. The hair styling was my contribution. The ladies would learn different ways to style their hair to compliment to their individual features. I would ask two ladies to come to my salon on the day of class. Every woman had different features. It was my job to bring out the best in each one. I would shampoo, shape with either a razor or scissor cut, set in sculpture curls and dry them under the dryer. They would then leave the salon with a net over their head and later, I would comb them out in front of the class.

I did the same for the women's clubs. Since each club met on different days of the month, this was ideal in helping to build my clientele. Within the year, my salon was at full capacity — complete with six operators, six dryers, two female assistants, and a receptionist that handled phone calls, appointments, and money.

My personal clientele was at 38 customers a day. I ran my business strict. Men wore white shirts, ties and cufflinks — they were the hairstylists. The other female assistants wore white uniforms. I trained my employees to concentrate only on the customer sitting in their chair. I never would allow a customer to be rushed because another one was waiting. Customers didn't mind, because they knew they were going to get top notch treatment when it was their turn. My salon had a reputation of having women walk out with beautiful hairstyles. When the boyfriends, husbands, or family members picked them up, they would always thanked me for making the woman beautiful.

I enjoyed being around women who took pride in their appearance. I had great satisfaction in that I played a part in building their self-esteem. I had the best of both worlds. I was successful and was surrounded by women.

There were days when a customer would walk in with a face that could stop a clock. She would hand me a magazine of a model with a beautiful hairstyle, and say, "I would like to have this style for me." I would tell her, "You have wonderful features that are unique to you. Why don't you let me give you a hairstyle that would accentuate your best attributes?" The glow on her face, when she looked in the mirror at the finished product, was worth the effort.

My salon operated, Monday through Friday from 9:00 a.m. to 2:00 a.m., and Saturdays from 7:00 a.m. to 5 p.m. I chose hours of operation convenient for woman who worked unconventional hours, especially those who worked at Teledyne Ryan, General Dynamics and Consolidated Aircraft.

One evening, I stopped by the Post Office to get my mail. I pulled out a letter from the United States Government. They were asking me to sign a waiver denouncing my disability so that the government could compensate less fortunate veterans.

Perhaps they wanted to forget what happened to me, but I'm reminded of it every day of my life. I worked hard to be where I am, so can they. I tore up the letter and threw it in the trash bin.

I was very proud of my growing business. My customers were the wives of prominent companies in San Diego, the Jewish community, the Madres – a group of dedicated women that traveled and supported the San Diego Padres, and The Powder Puffs – women aviators who flew cross country. I even had other beauty shop owners contact me to take care of their customers while they were on vacation.

I was the only hairstylist in San Diego that was a member of the Hollywood Hair Design Counsel. This solidified my reputation. I also joined the San Diego Cosmetologist Association - a state affiliated organization whereby, members had to be a hairdresser within the state of California. This recognition plaque gives a salon prestige. I was also a member of the Hairstyling Panel – a group of hairdressers that instructs and tests new products of that month at cosmetology schools throughout San Diego. If a product did not live up to its billings, the panel would not promote it.

Eventually, I became President of the San Diego Cosmetologist Association and the Hairstyling Panel. Now that I was settled in San Diego, I decided to move my mother and the kids to San Diego. I found them a house enrolled the kids in schools.

If my plate couldn't get any fuller, one day, Doris shows up at my beauty shop, alone. She needed my help. Perhaps if I gave the marriage another shot, I could help her get into a salon, earn a living, and bring Brad and Beverly down to San Diego so that we could all live together. I found her a salon in Coronado that had living quarters in the rear of the shop.

Business was going nicely for Doris and within a few months, she brought Brad and Beverly to San Diego. I rented an apartment for the four of us. For months, everything appeared to be working out. However, Brad was too hyper for Beverly.

One day, I received a phone call at the salon from my mother. Doris had dropped Brad off so she could watch him for the day. That evening, when I returned home, I found a note taped to the bathroom mirror. "Gone to San Francisco with Beverly." At that point I was finished. I closed the salon in Coronado and hired a live-in nanny, named Mae. She watched

Brad Monday through Saturday. Brad, a toddler now, got along well with her, but she would often tell me that he would tell her how much he missed his mother. Brad was a handful. He couldn't sit still and always wanted to climb on anything he could. He needed a lot of attention. On Saturdays, Mae would drop off Brad at the salon on her way home. Brad would spend the day at the salon with his coloring book and toys. Having my mother look after another child was not an option. The next day I contacted an attorney and filed for divorce.

During the week, Mae would tell me that Doris would call and want to speak with Brad. Brad wanted to be with his mother. He would cry and then she would hang up. I tried calling Doris but she would avoid my calls.

One afternoon, Mae phoned me at the salon, frantic. Doris had taken Brad. I had two customers under the dryer, at the time, and one in the chair. Since she already left, there wasn't anything I could do at that particular moment. I finished my customers and drove home to an empty house.

The next morning, I phoned my attorney and arranged for child support. Over time, phone calls to Brad were thwarted by the grandparents and Doris refused speak to me. When I did get an opportunity to speak with my son, our time on the phone was uncomfortable. I explained to him that I was doing the best I could to get him.

With the hours I was keeping, I chose to move in with my mother and the children. To pay for another place didn't make financial sense.

CHAPTER 14 – Meeting My Second Wife

The Hollywood Hair Design Counsel scheduled me to travel to Los Angeles and judge a hairstyling contest at the Ambassador Hotel. I ventured in the piano lounge and heard the most beautiful voice sing "Smoke Gets In Your Eyes." I found out that the lady singing, was named Joyce and she was with Betty Asian, an owner of a well-known beauty shop in La Jolla, CA. Betty knew of me and my salon in San Diego. I called her the next day and asked if I could have Joyce's phone number. Betty wanted to talk to Joyce first. If she was interested, than Betty would give me Joyce's phone number so I could call her. Within a week, we were on our first date.

A few months later, The Lafayette Hotel in San Diego was hosting the State Competition for Hair-Styling. I phoned Joyce and told her that I had won 1st place. She had Betty bring her over to the hotel so that we could celebrate together. She arrived dressed for the occasion. I had her accompany me for the picture holding the 1st place trophy.

Joyce and I continued to date. She had a daughter from a previous marriage, named Linda. I don't think she cared for me. Perhaps, I was taking too much time away from her relationship with her mother. She was an only child. Joyce lived with Betty, her husband, and 2 young daughters, Vicky and Jill. Fred, Betty's father, also lived there. At first, he didn't like me either. But one evening, Betty stuck up for me and said that I was somebody and that I could take care of Joyce and Linda. He begrudgingly agreed, but I could tell he still had reservations.

Whenever I'd arrive at Betty's house, Joyce was always cooking, cleaning, running the vacuum, and picking up after everyone. If the radio or stereo were playing, she would be singing along. One night over dinner, she shared with me that she had won numerous voice competitions and was offered a scholarship at The Julliard School in New York, to pursue a vocal career. She chose to be a mom to her daughter.

At Betty's house, I'd noticed everyone would just drop their clothes on the floor, or throw the dirty dishes in the sink. Joyce would always go behind and clean up after everyone. I felt the way she was treated was very degrading. However, you never heard her complain. I would enjoy taking Joyce out to dinner so she could have a break from the housework. Over dinner, we'd discuss our future together. One of our favorite places to dance was at the Lafayette Hotel. It had a supper club where you could have a nice dinner and then walk down a few stairs to the dance floor.

One day, Fred called me and said that all the furniture from his family in Kansas was at a storage facility in National City, a suburb of San Diego. If I paid the storage bill of $1500, Joyce could have all of her family's furniture. I was at the storage facility the next day and Joyce had her furniture.

Even though Joyce was happy, I could sense that Fred didn't like me. I couldn't let that bother me. I wanted to marry Joyce. One evening, Joyce called me frantically. She wanted me to come over right away. She was pregnant. Fred and Betty suggested an abortion in Tijuana, Mexico. However, I looked them both in the eyes, and said, "I love Joyce and I'll marry her." I have to wait until my divorce with Doris was final. My thoughts began to race. I wanted to be a better man than my father. I wasn't about to leave Joyce and let her fend for herself. This was my responsibility. As soon as my divorce was final from Doris, Joyce and I drove to Las Vegas and got married. Fred and Betty served as witnesses. Joyce, Linda and I settled in the North Park area of San Diego.

At that time, Wilford was graduating from Hoover High School. He was scheduled to receive a Varsity letter in Football at his senior banquet. That evening, I surprised him and sat with him at the banquet. After the ceremony, I approached Mr. Governelli, the football coach at San Diego State University. Wilford had talent on the field. I offered Mr. Governelli $75/ month for a scholarship so that Wilford could be on the football team. By the end of evening, Wilford had a four-year football scholarship complete with room and board.

Three months later, on August 19, 1955, Louis Alexander McKay.Jr., born. He weighed 4 pounds. 6 ounces. I remember Joyce saying that he was such an easy delivery. That was a good thing, because this baby had colic like you wouldn't believe. The lung capacity of an infant is mind boggling. In amidst being new parents together, it wasn't easy. We were not able to take Louis home, because he was too small. Babies had to weigh 6 pounds in order to be released from the hospital. He was such a tiny little boy. Joyce would say he looked like a little fish. When Louis finally gained enough weight to leave the hospital, he let everyone know in no uncertain terms, how happy he was to be going home. It seemed that every time I saw Louis, Jr., he was crying.

I still felt Linda resented having to share her mother with other people. Wilma and Rose needed me, since neither of them could drive at that time. The location of my mother's house was convenient for the girls could walk to their schools. I was still sending support for Brad and worked hard to maintain the business.

Since this was my chosen path, and I was going to make it work.

We all managed to survive. Louis Jr, was very cute and very hyper. He was into everything. And if he wasn't included in everything, he cried because his feelings got hurt so easily. I remember when I took Joyce to beauty events, and Louis would get upset when we left.

When we arrived home that evening, Linda who was taking care of Louis Jr.,and would tell us that he cried so hard and for so long, that he vomited all over his walker, screen door, and the surrounding floor. Changing him was always a risky situation. When I'd make him laugh, he'd smile and then pee would shoot up in my face. He giggled every time it happened. His colic finally began to subside and he appeared a happier little boy.

On the business front, the salon was growing and operators were building their clientele. I would go to the beauty school, located within the US Grant Hotel on Broadway. I respected the way the director handled her beauty school. Her reputation spoke for itself — 98% of her students passed the State Board. I also liked the fact that she didn't accept every applicant. The director would allow me to oversee the potential stylist. This way, I could observe their talent, demeanor, and how they treated the person sitting in their chair. I learned everything I needed to know by watching them at work. I'd get their name, jot it down on a tablet. I then, made arrangements with the director to call me and let me know when my selected students graduated and passed the State Board. She'd give me their phone number and I'd call them and invite them to the salon for an interview.

Recruiting an operator right out of beauty school meant they hadn't developed bad habits. I would teach them the foundation of hairstyling. Once they mastered the art of reading a person's features, they could create their own unique hairstyles to complement each and every customer. I wanted operators who wanted to do good work, and enjoyed helping one another so they could develop their own clientele. Everyone in my salon had a mindset to succeed, if not, I'd give them their walking papers.

On the home-front, conflicts with Doris in San Francisco regarding Brad escalated. However, I continued to remain in contact and send support.

Within a few short months, Joyce became pregnant again. Eleven months later, on July 5, 1956, Lance Atkins McKay was born. Lance was completely different then Louis, Jr. He was born asleep. He was so relaxed, the doctors would reassure Joyce that he was healthy and not to worry.

Joyce would say, "Thank goodness they both aren't going to be walking at the same time or I'd really have my hands full."

Lance was very sweet and sensitive. He never cried unless he was hungry or wanted his diaper changed. If you left him in his crib and he wanted to get out, he wouldn't scream for attention. You would walk into the bedroom and he would have his head on the railing, pouting. He was very sweet little boy. Over time, even though the boys couldn't communicate with

each other, you could tell they were going to have a special
relationship.

*Thanks San Diego Honor Flight for
making this possible for WW II Veterans.
My picture at the Washington DC , World
War II Memorial. Left to right two
veterans Myself , Colleen my niece Sam
in the stroller and my brother Wilford
and Colleen's partner Nadine...*

CHAPTER 15 – My First Son Returns Home

One day, I called the grandparents to speak to my son and they wouldn't tell me where he was. Doris wasn't there and I went ahead and left a message knowing she wouldn't call me back. I became concerned as this continued for several days. I contacted an attorney requested that he do some research. He found out that Brad had been taken to an orphanage in San Francisco. My attorney filed a court order that enabled me to pick up Brad and bring him to San Diego to live with me.

I sat Joyce down and explained to her my decision. Without hesitation, she encouraged me to fly to San Francisco and get my son. When I arrived, I drove over to the orphanage, presented the court order to the nun, and demanded my son.

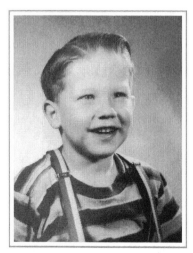 

Bradford Douglas McKay

Brad walked out the building bewildered. I took his hand and we drove to the airport and boarded a plane to San Diego. I noticed that Brad kept looking out the window of the airplane and was silent the entire flight home. I told him, "You're coming to live with me and my family." He never muttered a word. When we arrived home, Joyce was at the front door expecting us both.

I took hold of Brad's hand, and said, "This is your new mom and this is your home." Joyce welcomed my son, introduced him to Linda, Louis, Jr., and Lance, and showed him around the house. It was apparent that he was shy, uncomfortable and confused. Coming out of orphanage a few hours prior, all I wanted to do was welcome him into a stable home environment, once and for all.

Linda was another story. She didn't want to share her mother with anyone. And the more kids that demanded more of her mother's attention meant less for her. This stems back to when I entered Joyce's life. Growing up, this girl was the only child. Fred Atkins gave her whatever she wanted and she could do whatever she wanted. Things were different now. Linda was part of a family, good, bad or indifferent. You have to share, pick up after yourself and help out with all the members of the family.

Brad enrolled in school and appeared to have adjusted to a routine. However, his nervous energy was difficult to for him to control.

Needless to say, Joyce had her hands full with Brad and Linda not getting along. I was hoping, in time, they would get to like one another. The important thing was that Brad was in a good home. Brad liked the boys and he helped Joyce with them.

"Louis Jr., a character," Joyce would always say, "He sure keeps me on my toes." When Lance would use his training walker, Louis would always want to play. They would always want to be within an ear shot of one another. What one didn't think of the other one did.

Wooden play-pens were used back in the 1950s. The boys could play with their toys and not get into trouble. This gave Joyce a chance to have a break from the kids so she could either cook or do housework.

However, Joyce's break didn't last long. When Lance was eight months old, we found out that she was pregnant once again. Soon, test revealed that we were going to have a little girl. Wilford was about to begin his junior year at SDSU, Wilma her senior year at Hoover High School, and Rose, her junior year.

Linda and Brad were still in elementary school and doing well. Fortunately, their school was within walking distance from our home. Brad and Linda were adjusting to they're growing family. Wilma wanted to venture into the Beauty Business. I told her that once she graduated from High School, I would pay for her tuition. Rose began playing the Viola in the school orchestra. She was very independent and a go-getter. As a junior, I had no doubt Rose would succeed on her own.

I remember Lance's first birthday. Joyce had placed him on the dining room table so he could blow out a candle on his cake. He proceeded to put his feet and face in the cake and frosting and laugh until everyone in the room was laughing equally as hard. Joyce finally threw up her hands and said, "Let's take a picture."

I noticed that this third pregnancy was not as easy for Joyce. The doctor told us that the lining in Joyce's stomach needed to heal. After this pregnancy, no more kids. She was tired and my schedule was still hectic. With Linda helping her mother and Brad helping out with the boys, we all survived and persevered. On December 13, 1957, Lisa Ann McKay was born. She was a good baby. Joyce would often say she wasn't demanding.

As the kids grew older, it was nice to see everyone get along. The boys were still getting into whatever they could. The boys enjoyed putting on their sleepers and holsters and play cowboys.

Joyce would always make sure that everyone was in their Sunday best for church. Jumpsuits and dresses were always pressed.

When Lisa started to walk, she always wanted to dress up and have her picture taken. She would often accompany Joyce at Joyce hair appointments, so that I could give her a hair-do. Lisa was as polite as she was cute. Joyce would purchase Stride-Rites and leather training shoes from Walker Scott. Back then, you wore good shoes to help mold your feet.

One day, I came home from work, and Joyce told me that she had to put bells on the boys shoe laces so she could keep track of them out of the corner of her eyes. She would say, "When I don't hear those bells, those boys are into something."

The play-pen was a life saver for Joyce as she would use it for naps or when she had to tend to the kids separately. At the end of day, Joyce would say, "Somebody always needs their diaper changed." Two kids in diapers and one on his way into training pants, the toilet bowls were busy.

I wasn't able to play with the toddlers as often as I would have liked. By the time I finished my day, everyone was asleep and my dinner was waiting in the oven.

I looked forward to Sundays. It was a day for church, Sunday dinner, and a chance to relax, rejuvenate and spend time with the family. I wanted the kids to have a religious foundation.

One day, I made an appointment with the priest at St. Patrick's Catholic Church. I inquired about Joyce becoming a Catholic. He told me it would cost me $500. With that, I walked out and my family and I never returned to that church again.

When Wilma graduated from Hoover, she attended beauty school. When she graduated and passed the State Board, she came to work with me in my hair styling salon. I helped her build her clientele and I conducted hair-coloring contests for the

Miss Clairol product line for 1500 hairdressers throughout San Diego County. She won a 1st place. Also in recognition of National Beauty Salon Week, there were contests for women aged 70 and older, held every year and throughout the state of California. During that week, I would provide complimentary haircuts to bedridden patients in hospitals throughout San Diego. When I arrived, the head nurse would hand me a list of the patients that I was to see. As it would turn out, I would lift the spirits of someone in dire need.

It didn't take long for Wilma to build her clientele. It was a rewarding feeling for me to see her begin her career as a hairdresser and blossom into a hairstylist. Within the year Wilma wanted to work for another beauty salon. Soon, Wilford, Wilma and Rose married and ventured on a life of their own. Since my mother didn't drive, I was the one to look after her and make sure she still had the things she needed. When operators would leave to go elsewhere to start their own beauty shops, they would take their clientele with them. This impacted profits and forced me to start over again and hire a new staff.

The expense of raising my family was constant and soon began to take its financial and emotional toll. Patience was still an arduous task. Having mastered hair design, I was now able to control the strength in my hands. However, I still would not tolerate those who would disrespect me or my operators. I would say, "You just got yourself a free shampoo and set, please don't come back."

One afternoon I had a heart-to-heart talk with one of my customers while I was doing her hair. She was a nurse's aid while I was recovering from my war wounds at the San Diego Naval Hospital. It had become apparent to her over time, that I was overwhelmed. She would often wonder how I did it all.

She used to hear me sing with the radio while I was at the US Naval Hospital. She suggested voice lessons as a hobby in addition to hairstyling.

I contacted a voice teacher by the name of Mrs. Spears, and began taking vocal lessons. Singing was a great outlet. Learning the mechanics of singing didn't seem like work. I enjoyed every minute. Unfortunately, my lessons didn't last long as my teacher's husband was transferred to Guam.

I then contacted the head of the music department at SDSU, they recommended Mr. Raul Couyas. He was a resident voice teacher for students. I had a voice lesson once a week. He trained me as a dramatic tenor and I memorized lead tenor roles in four operas.

Joyce was busy at home raising five kids and I was busy making a living. We didn't even have time to think about having anymore children until Joyce started to feel sick again. She used to say, "I have that feeling again, Louis." We made an appointment with the doctor and found out she was expecting. We thought that we had all the kids we going to have, since Lisa was such a hard delivery for Joyce. Her stomach lining was very weak and from the onset, we knew that this pregnancy was going to be difficult. Thank goodness, Brad and Linda were teenagers and a great help to the family. Brad looked after the boys and Linda looked after Lisa.

One day, in the newspaper, I read that a director, by the name of Carl Dewse, needed 1000 voices to sing for a Billy Graham religious revival held at Balboa Stadium in San Diego. I auditioned and was accepted into the choir as a Baritone. The evening of the revival was invigorating and rewarding. I felt a sense of euphoria singing amongst a choir of 1000 voices. Mr. Dewse and I got along great. I found out that he was also a choir director and vocal coach at University Christian Church. I decided to work with Mr. Dewse. My family began to attend University Christian Church. All the kids attended Sunday school and the church service.

Soon Joyce was about to give birth. She was very uncomfortable, as this was a very difficult pregnancy for her, and was tired. On December 5, 1960, Joyce gave birth to Lita Adele McKay.

During delivery, she hemorrhaged. This made it very difficult for the baby to get oxygen and the doctors were concerned he would lose both Joyce and the baby. Gangrene started to set in and it made a bad situation worse. Joyce was hospitalized for 31 days, administered 10 blood transfusions and at times wasn't expected to live. I remember one day the doctor pulled me aside and said, "If this woman gets pregnant one more time, she will die." The next day, I scheduled an appointment for a vasectomy. With the help of Aunt Betty, Linda and whoever could help, the house and children were taken care of and Joyce was finally able to come home. It took Joyce months to recover emotionally and physically. Her body, was just too tired, but, she persevered. I've never known a tougher woman.

We eventually moved to a larger house in the Banker's Hill. The landlady was reluctant to rent to such a large family. So, Joyce suggested they come and see how she kept house with six children, and then make their decision. Once they saw how immaculate our house was with all of the antiques, they agreed to let us rent to own with first option to buy. Soon we were settled in.

It was a three story home complete with an attic and basement was the entire length of the house. There was a 10 foot gold-leaf mirror against the wall of the foyer as you walked in, and it had a very large front room, a mahogany paneled dining room with beveled glass built-Ins, a very large kitchen with a butler's pantry, a den with a laid marble floor and four bedroom. In the back yard was a covered gazebo with a built-in fireplace, four large avocado trees, two lemon trees, a large tiled fountain in the middle of the yard, and a granny flat complete with a bathroom and kitchenette, above the garage , all for the grand price of $155/month.

It cost a fortune to heat the place and took a year to pay off each Christmas. Heck, we gave gifts to everyone, even the mailman, and we had a fresh 12-foot Noble tree every year.

Every time I'd walk in the house, I would turn off the heat and unnecessary lights and Joyce would come in behind me and turn them back on.

When Lita was little, Joyce and I would take her to places with us. She'd snuggle in a big chair, and if it was around her bed time, she'd be fast asleep in no time. She had the same opportunities as everyone else. Lita always helped and looked after her mother — always offering to help the other brothers and sisters. Growing up, perhaps she learned from the other kids what worked and what didn't.

One morning, on the way to church, Lisa shut the car door on four of my fingers. This made hairstyling very difficult and solidified the need for another occupation in order to make a living.

Lisa did well in school. One day, her elementary school had the yearly musical program. Joyce and I didn't know anything about it until the last minute. All of sudden she moved out in front of the school choir and began to sing her solo. Joyce and I had no idea she was even going to be in the program, let alone, sing. She did a wonderful job. She also showed a talent for drawing. She sketched and painted water colors beautifully.

She would often say she wanted to be an art teacher when she grew up.

One day, a gentleman was walking through the neighborhood and offered to take pictures of the kids of the neighborhood on top of a pony. Therefore, our children had their pictures taken in a full cowboy or cowgirl outfit.

We even had Linda's wedding reception at the house. Linda had it made. Louis and Lance were ring-bearers, Lisa and Lita were the flower girls and Vicki and Jill were in the bridal party. I think we had over 150 people.

When Lisa was about 10, she was run over by a car on her way to the neighborhood store. A car had stopped so Lisa could walk across, but a carpet cleaning truck swerved around the stopped car and hit Lisa. I was notified about the car accident while at a rehearsal for an upcoming opera and rushed to meet Joyce at the hospital. Lisa recovered, but her personality was different. When she woke up she had no idea as to why she was there. She became withdrawn and quiet and was never the same. She was very nervous and had a short temper. The sweet girl that we all knew and loved changed.

Lita was introduced to music and began taking piano lessons at 9 years-old. To pay for them, I prepared three custom wigs every week for her lessons. Lita continued with her piano lessons through junior high. In addition, she participated in track and field and also choir.

With the boys getting involved in baseball, Brad helped out and coached the teams at Challenge Field in Mission Valley. He would tell me about Lance playing center field. He complained that he would count the number the cars going by on the Highway 8, instead paying attention to the game and the opposing team at bat.

Brad was still hyper, so the busier he was the better. The three boys would never tell on each other. Unfortunately, when one got into trouble, all three got the belt.

One day, Louis, Jr., came home from work. He said that the neighbor's son behind us offered him and Lance Marijuana. Later that day, I called the young boy over to the fence and said, "If you ever offer my boys any drugs of any kind again, I'll kill you." Things were never the same with our neighbors.

Even with the hours I was keeping, I wanted my family to know that if they needed me, I was a phone call away.

Brad wanted to play football in high school, but unfortunately, he hurt his right knee before the start of his junior year, and right before his senior year, he hurt his left leg. This put him out for the entire season. He was devastated.

After graduation, Brad moved out to live with a girlfriend. Since, I was told after the fact, this infuriated me. My main concern was to keep a roof over my family's head and food on the table — be it good, bad, or indifferent. Even though I was busy outside the house, I expected to be a part of every decision that impacted my kids and my household. I became increasingly disappointed that Joyce would make decisions and not tell me until later or when something would happen.

Soon, Brad returned home and told us that he wanted to join the Army. I sat him down and gave him the best advice I could, "Obey the rules and be quick about it. If they tell you to hit the deck, do it. That will save your life in combat."

CHAPTER 16 My Time With The San Diego Starlight Opera

Also, in the trunk, is stack of Starlight Opera programs bound together. Sifting through them all brings back memories. I'm touched that my mother had saved each and everyone. My time with Starlight Opera Company started back when I heard that they were holding auditions for their upcoming summer season. The performances are held in historic Balboa Park, a beautiful area in the central part of San Diego next to the world renowned Organ Pavilion and the San Diego Aerospace Museum. I auditioned and was given a role of the father in "Brigadoon."

One season, I auditioned for the role as the Innkeeper in "The Student Prince." I noticed that there were a lot of kids in the summer productions of Starlight. I wanted to introduce Louis and Lance to the stage. It meant that I would be able to spend time with them and ensure that they would have a fulfillment later in life. Since I knew my way around Starlight, I knew who to go to for advice on having my kids audition.

Louis and Lance received chorus parts in the beginning. Louis's first role was Amal, in "Amal And The Night Visitors."

This exposure enabled him to move into supporting roles in future productions, and ultimately a leading role as "Oliver, in Oliver Twist." Although, Lance and Louis spent a great deal of time together on stage, Lance was happy just to be around Louis and the rest of the chorus. Although, Lance took voice lessons, his interest in pursuing singing was later in life. Lance was a roughneck, an outdoorsman good at sports.

When I picked up the entertainment section of the morning newspaper, I noticed that Louis auditioned and obtained the lead role as "Oliver." It happened to be Louis Jr.'s, 12th birthday, while he was on stage. I remember taking my entire family to the Civic Theater for opening night. At the end of the performance, the backstage crew rolled out an enormous cake. The cast, orchestra and audience of over 2900 people sang "Happy Birthday."

During my workday, I remember getting phone calls from Joyce telling me the boys were misbehaving. In the evenings, she would be so upset, but didn't want me to touch them. Other times, I would have to punish then for misbehaving even though I hadn't seen them for a couple of days.

One evening, Joyce and I laughed after she told me that the kids were playing ball in the house. Although it was humorous, she wanted me to go upstairs and talk to the boys. Because I hadn't seen much of them lately, once they arrived in the bedroom, I had each of them pick up a shoebox and let me hit it with the belt. I told them to scream as loud as they could. Finally, after hearing screams coming from the kids for an about a minute, Joyce threw open the door, "Louis, Sr., don't you ever touch those kids again. You're going to kill them." All of us just stood there and laughed hysterically.

On a serious note, there were many times when I gave my kids the belt, backhanded them and knocked them onto the floor. It was hard for me to control my temper. Even today, I have to keep it in check. My kids knew, without a doubt, that I would not tolerate disrespect towards their mother or me. You never turn your nose up at meals. If you don't like what is being prepared, you do without or stay in the kitchen until finished.

I just shake my head in amazement when I realize how busy I was and how many directions I ventured in to make a living. When times were good, I shared it. I would not only feed my family, but the friends of my kids. They would come over after school and since my wife was always home for our kids, they wanted to be there. It often got to the point where I joked around and said, "You again, I'm going to start charging you rent." Even though it was expensive, there's a positive side — our kids were home.

We hosted backyard BBQ's for Brad's cap league, the boy's little league and pony league, the girl's brownie and girls scouts, cub scout and starlight cast parties. Having gatherings at our house, meant that our kids were home and not wandering elsewhere. It seemed like a small price to pay for peace of mind.

Even during the most hectic times in my life, I tried to spend time with the family. Having a wife who didn't drive, and if my schedule permitted, I would take the kids to the little league, watch wrestling matches, or take the boys on camping trips, take one of the girls to piano lessons or her first fishing trip. Other family members helped out when my schedule didn't allow me to be there. Saturdays, after my long workday, I would grocery shop for the family. When I arrived home with a carload of groceries, the kids created an assembly line as they carried in the groceries. Every child took part in the family unit. Joyce made

Saturdays a day for house cleaning and yard work. Only when the chores were done, were you allowed to go out and play.

Louis continued to excel in music. One day, I took him to an audition for a dance group called the Bright Side. During the audition, Don Ward, the director, turned to me and said, "It's too bad your son has two left feet and doesn't have much rhythm." I didn't pay any attention to him. The next day, they called Louis and told him he was a natural, and he joined the Bright Side.

Both boys were members of the High School Choir and lettered in various sports; Lance Football, Basketball and Wrestling and Louis - Gymnastics and Wrestling.

Soon after Louis Jr., graduated from High School, he studied dance and theatre in Los Angeles and auditioned for the Debbie Reynolds Show that was scheduled to open in Las Vegas. He became her chief choreographer.

When it came time for Louis to leave Las Vegas, Debbie asked him to teach the routines to a new dancer. "Who walks in, Don Ward's son!" It's interesting how life unfolds. Louis moved back to San Diego, and opened his own dance company.

Lance graduated from High School and pursued a career in Real Estate and has been successful at it ever since.

Lisa also enjoyed music as well. She joined the choir in junior high and took piano lessons and played by ear. Throughout high school, Lisa was rebellious and eager to leave the house. Since she had enough credits to graduate early, it would only be a matter of time before she was on her own.

I'm very grateful that our kids grew up in the era that they did. Kids playing Hide 'n Seek until the street lights came on, playing outside without a fear of being taken by a stranger, never having to lock the doors to our home, making your own fun with slip 'n slide while your mom hosed down the plastic as you slid down the front lawn, attaching cards with clothes pins to the spokes of your bike, and watching out for your neighbor and their kids because it was the thing to do.

Kids had to make their own fun. There were no computer games and our kids didn't sit around and watch television. Once they finished their homework, they went outside to play until they were called in for dinner. They had chores without an allowance. When the boys had their friends over for dinner, I was very strict. You abide by the rules in my house as if you

155

were mine. Friends didn't disrupt our household routine. If they didn't like the rules they could leave and not come back. Having our kids grow up the way they did, hopefully makes them appreciate the way life used to be.

My family:Louis A. McKay Jr.,Linda Birkeland, Joyce,,Lance A. McKay, Lita Arvizu, Louis A. McKay Sr.,, Bradford Douglas McKay, Lisa McKay.

CHAPTER 17 – Earning My Masters Degree

As I sit here looking at a Trophy on a table from "Annie Get Your Gun," I smile. I played the role of "Chief Sitting Bull." The cast wanted to treat the Chief like any other Indian. However, I felt that role deserved dignity and respect. The director agreed and created a dance for Annie and Sitting Bull. It brought the house down.

In the formative days of the San Diego Grand Opera Company, operas were sung in English. In the newspaper, this opera company was holding auditions for the chorus. During the audition, I had the pleasure of meeting the rehearsal pianist, Ilana Mysior. What a talent! I auditioned and became a member of the chorus with the San Diego Opera. My mother saved every program I had given her. I asked for the director's permission to stand in the wings and observe how the artists would apply their craft. This provided me the insight into the creative world of an actor-singer.

I had the privilege of watching Norman Treigl, a Bass, Placido Domingo, a Tenor, and Beverly Sills, a Coloratura Soprano (the very highest soprano). I watched their every move and took mental notes on how they made their roles come to life. Illana later became my coach in learning my comprimario roles. Camprimario roles are third in line; lead, supporting and then a camprimario role. It was during my private lessons with her that I learned she was also on the faculty in the music department at the University of San Diego.

I trained for comprimario roles in addition to singing in the chorus. At the time, lead and supporting roles were brought in from Europe. The benefit of singing both was that I received two paychecks per rehearsal and two paychecks per performance. This enabled me to make ends meet at the salon. The business was struggling and operators were leaving to start their own businesses.

The city of San Diego changed Fifth Avenue to a north bound one-way and removed the bus stop. This devastated my business. The depression hit hard. The income for the salon dwindled from $80-100/day to $4/day. You would hear of people leaving their homes and cars with the keys in them. You would read about people who left San Diego or traveled back to their home town to live with their parents or in-laws. Some of these people were my customers. They would tell me that they couldn't make it in San Diego. I'd see people drive cars up and down Fifth Avenue with a megaphone saying, "Buy a car, save the economy." The beauty business was no longer lucrative.

I decided to turn my beauty salon into a music studio. I had my mother's piano moved over to the salon so that I could teach voice. I had two students that excelled in voice — a girl from National City named Rica, who auditioned and landed the lead role in "Saigon," on Broadway. She still lives in New York today and is doing great. The other student was Joel, a boy from San Carlos, who went on to become a Baritone soloist with the San Diego and Orange County Opera Company.

The relationship between Joyce and I became strained. She thought that if I would stay in the shop, hire more people, I wouldn't have to get other work and be gone as much. But this wasn't the case. I began to feel isolated. Important decisions regarding our home that should have involved the two of us working together didn't happen. She continued informing me about situations after they occurred.

I continued to enjoy teaching and singing. I would perform at local Convalescent and retirement homes once a week and sing an hour of old songs from the 40's-50's.

One visit stands out in my memory. After I finished singing, I noticed this lady sitting by herself. Her face looked so incredibly sad. I asked her if she had a favorite song that I could sing for her the next time I visited. She said she liked the songs I sang, and it didn't matter. I couldn't get over the sadness in her face. She proceeded to tell me that her son put her there and hadn't come to visit her.

On the way out, I asked the director of the facility for the son's phone number so I could call him. I contacted the son and told him that his mother needed to see him and that she missed him terribly. His response was, "I can't be around someone who is disabled." I asked him, "Do you want to be disabled, because if you do, I can take a baseball bat to your knees and help you out." There was silence on the other end.

The next time I visit your mother, and she tells me that you haven't come to see her, "I'm paying you a visit." The next time I performed, I walked up to her. She was smiling, and before I had a chance to ask her about her son. She said, "He came to visit me and I'm so happy." Mission accomplished. It was therapeutic for me to give of my time.

One day, Mr. Herbert, the director of the San Diego Opera Company, called me to his office. He informed me that I would not get any more camprimario roles because I didn't have a music degree from an accredited college. He mentioned San Diego State College. However, I wanted to go to the University of San Diego and have the opportunity to work with Illana.

Then, I went to the Veteran's Administration and received information regarding my GI Bill. I had six months left of assistance. The nice thing about the GI Bill is that you don't need to repay the loan and it gives veterans an opportunity for an education. I spoke with registrar's office and was told I needed to have my high school transcript. Once again, I contacted Joe E. Carlson. It was to rekindle our friendship that had grown dear over the years. He was doing well and always asked about my family.

A week later, the admissions office contacted me, and gave me some disappointing news, my "C" average grades in high school did not meet their requirements for admission. However, they would reconsider their decision if I would submit a letter explaining my reasons for wanting to attend the University and obtain a degree in Music. I stated that in order for me to pursue a career in the opera, I had to have a degree in music. I know I didn't play an instrument. However, I did love to sing.

My acceptance to the University was contingent on having a "B" average by the second semester, or I would be dropped. I agreed to the terms, received student loans in order to help pay for tuition and supplies and started my freshman year in September, 1974. The Veterans were going to pay for six months of my education. By the end of second semester, I had a "B" average.

At this point, my marriage to Joyce was one of co-existence. Although she understood that my degree in music would enhance my earning potential, she wanted me to spend more time at home, now that we only had one child left. However, I was only going to be around until Lita finished high school. In the summer, I attended Cal Western and studied music under Dr. Teutch, head of the music department. This enabled me to transfer eight units over to USD and help with my music requirement.

I remember preparing for an upcoming audition for the role of the "Lamplighter," in the world premier of the "Young Lord" by the San Diego Opera Company. In preparing for this role, I found out that music score was not available in the United States. I contacted Thearl's Music Store and they found a copy in Germany and ordered it for me. When the music arrived, I remember looking at the three inch thick score. How was I going to learn my role in English when it was written in German, and in enough time to audition by fall? Dr. Teutch translated the score from German to English. As soon as I received it, I brought it over to Illana and we studied in time for me to audition. Mr. Herbert was so impressed that I had someone translate my role to English that I was given the part on the spot.

Attending college at 51 was a commitment that would pave the way for me to be a part of the opera. My favorite courses were religion and music. The music curriculum required that I learn to play an instrument. I decided to take piano. I also entered the Sister Rossi contest for music majors. I sang and won 1st place.

One day, I read in the newspaper that Mr. Herbert had passed away. I had lost a very important person in my life. He was my friend and no one will be able to replace him. He was my mentor in singing for the San Diego Opera Company.

A man by the name of Tito Capobianco took over this position and did away with anyone that was working or had worked with Mr. Herbert. The only staff he kept was the stage crew. This closed the door for me with the San Diego Opera Company. However, I continued with my education.

During my senior year, upper division music classes also fulfilled a portion of the degree requirement towards a Master's program in education. I graduated in May, 1978 with a BA in Music and continued to pursue a Master's degree in Bilingual Cross Culture.

Since Lita was in her junior year at San Diego High School, we had to start applying to Universities and Colleges. She was accepted at USD starting in the fall of 1979. My Veteran's educational benefits helped pay for her education. Lita graduated from High School in 1979 and began her education at USD.

My Master's degree would enable me to teach music and Spanish in the public schools — grades K-12 and also teach at a two year junior college level. Once I passed the required tests, I received my California State teaching credential in Music, Cross Culture, and Bilingual Education.

It was during this time that my marriage with Joyce deteriorated. Sadly, we had already drifted apart. She even had one of my son's surprise me at school to see if I was studying. Joyce didn't trust me. I made more money singing than I ever did as a hairstylist. I wanted to do something different with my life and Joyce refused to accept that.

One evening, at the salon, I was visiting with one of my customers. While she was there, I received a phone call from a loan company. If I didn't come in and pay $500, Joyce would lose our furniture that I had used as collateral. My customer offered to lend me the money. I put the check in my pocket and we continued to visit. All of sudden, Joyce bursts through the door and yanks the customer off the stairs. I tried to explain too Joyce that nothing was going on but she refused to listen. She felt that if I spent more time in the shop, I'd make money.

A couple of weeks later, I ran into Linda's father-in-law on his way to work. He proceeded to tell me that Linda and his son, asked him to loan them money so that they could purchase the house in Banker's Hill.

I was shocked and didn't believe him. I drove home and confronted Joyce. She told me it didn't matter because I didn't have the money. I demanded to see the paperwork. I called my cousin, Sergio, an attorney, and told him of the situation. He agreed to lend me $20,000 to buy the house. I took the paperwork to the Realty company and demanded they give me the mandatory 10 days to come up with the money. They informed me that they made a personal visit to Joyce and told her she had 10 days to respond and that the allotted time had already expired. When I arrived home, Joyce was still upset about the other night and we had words. She said, "You don't have the guts to leave." With that, I grabbed my things and left.

I filed for divorce and things got very ugly between us. Joyce had to move into a tiny 2 bedroom home and had to sell a lot of her furniture and I moved over to my mother's home. She was staying with Wilma at that time. I felt angry and betrayed that she would allow us to lose the home. The beauty of this property was that it included a four-unit apartment complex located on the street behind our house.

Today, the property is worth over $2.5 million. All that was required for payment at the time was $20,000. The divorce dragged on for several years. My side of the family didn't speak with her side of the family and the kids didn't have anything to do with me. When I lost the house, I lost my family. Looking back, it was probably very uncomfortable for the kids. The kids defended and looked after their mother. I was now an outsider. However, I continued to pay for Joyce's alimony and contributed to her expenses.

__Displayed at the Douglas Historical Society Museum.__
My four year lettermen sweater in Football, Baseball and Basketball and Musical Insignia.

CHAPTER 18 – Finding Myself In Time of Need

By 1981, I was a substitute teacher. I chose San Diego and, Sweetwater Unified School Districts. This new avenue of income made it possible to sell my beauty salon and devote my time to teaching. Since I wanted flexibility with my time, and teach all over the county, I chose to be a substitute teacher. That way, I had the opportunity to interact with students of all ages and different grade levels.

At times I worked five days a week. Other times, I taught a couple of times a week. However, I never taught the same class more than three days in a row. Teaching enabled me to start paying off my education loans to the tune of $156,000.

Being the teacher rather than the student gave me a bird's eye view into how the schools and our educational system had changed over the years. The lack of respect the students had for their teachers was very disappointing. In my opinion, a teacher is a teacher. It doesn't matter if he or she is a substitute. Many students thought that because I was their substitute, they didn't have to follow the lesson plan or my rules. I wasn't a glorified babysitter. I was there to teach. When a student disrupted one of my classes, I gave them a pass to the library and an "F" on the attendance sheet. I even asked if there were any other students that wanted to go along. It wasn't fair to the students who were in class to learn. That way, the lesson plan that was left for me to follow, I completed by the end of the day and everyone was content.

Within a short time, my reputation followed me and word spread. I rarely had a problem with students from that point on.

I remember one incident at Chula Vista High School, where I dismissed six disruptive students from my class. I gave each of them a pass to the library and an "F" for the day. Soon, the Vice-Principal showed up and wanted to know why the students were sent to the library. I explained to him what happened and he told me I had to let the students back in the class. I said, "You bring them back, I leave and you can take over the class." The students didn't return and the lesson plans were completed.

In contrast, the kids in grades K-3 were eager to learn and enjoyed being at school. Watching the kids interact with one another made for a very pleasurable experience.

My mother's health began to deteriorate and she had to be hospitalized for poor circulation and high blood pressure. When she was ready to be released, I phoned Wilma and requested a meeting. I needed her to help care for our mother. My mother wanted to live with Rose. However, Rose's husband wanted his mother to live with them.

Within the week, Wilma and her husband, showed up at our apartment with a moving truck and took everything except a cot and a television. My mother moved to Wilma's home in Tustin where she had people to look after her.

For the first time in my life, I didn't have to worry about my mother's care or anyone for that matter.

Fortunately, Joel Snyder, a past student of mine, was looking for a place to live at the time. We became roommates. He was busy singing for the Opera Pacific in Orange County and I was busy teaching.

One day, after school, I had a message on my phone from the Audition Chairman from the Opera Pacific. He wanted to know if I would be interested in auditioning for the company. I made an appointment for the next day, and when I finished my Aria in Italian, was hired.

With the flexibility of my teaching schedule and evening choral rehearsals, I tackled both for a number of years. Joel would drive his car one day and I would drive the next. During the evening drives home, we would turn on the radio and listen to "Bill Balance."

One day, at school, a student of mine came up to me during recess and wondered if my voice was hurting me because I sounded hoarse. Recently, I too had noticed my voice sounding raspy. However, I thought that I was simply over-using my voice.

When I finally paid off my student loans and the opera pay started to exceed substitute teaching, I declined more teaching assignments and devoted more of my time in Orange County. Sadly, my mother passed away in 1992. My mother had requested I sing her favorite Spanish songs at her funeral. Joyce and the kids attended the funeral, and our communication was brief — one of expressing their condolences. After the service, I remember walking to the open casket and sobbing. She was wearing the sterling silver locket that I made for her when I was a Silver-Smith.

My relationship with Wilford, Wilma and Rose ceased with my mother passing away. They didn't call me and I didn't call them. If they had a problem with how I was caring for my mother, they should have taken the time out of their busy schedules to help instead of always depending on me to do it for them.

I continued to sing with the Opera Pacific for a number of years and Joel decided to move to Orange County.

For me, the commute and traffic began to take its toll. My throat began to tire easily and I couldn't seem to get rid of this odd-tight feeling, no matter how much I gargled with warm salt water.

During the last performance of "Turandot," the annoying tight feeling in my throat persisted. The next day, I made an appointment with my regular doctor and she referred me to a throat specialist at the Veteran's Hospital in La Jolla. After numerous tests, they found cancer on the bottom of my right vocal chord. The doctor suggested laser to remove the cancer so as to preserve the chord.

Unfortunately, the laser treatment missed the cancerous growth because it had grown underneath the right vocal cord. I turned to a private ear, nose and throat specialist to direct me to the appropriate facility that administers chemotherapy and radiation treatments. Fortunately, there was a facility minutes away from my home. Although I had to pay out of pocket for the treatments, I didn't mind. I had lost confidence in the VA when the previous treatment failed. I tried to remain positive and not let thoughts of defeat enter my mind. I felt fortunate because the cancer had not spread. I put myself in the hands of the specialist. Whatever the outcome, it was meant to be.

The day of the first treatment, a clear lightweight brace was fitted on the sides of my head to prevent any movement. My head was the only part of my body in the radiation machine. The treatment was painless and only lasted, what seemed like a few seconds. When the area responded favorably, the doctor scheduled 30 consecutive treatments.

In the beginning, I was still able to eat and drink. However, the more treatments I received, it felt like I had something caught in my throat. It wasn't painful, just uncomfortable.

At the end of my 30 treatments, the cancer was destroyed and the year of healing began. I scheduled monthly visits to see the specialist to ensure the cancer had not returned.

The doctor told me that I would be hoarse and my voice would never be the same — a small price to pay for being alive. My quest was to get rid of what could have taken my life if left untreated. So, I had limited use of my voice. I still had my life and I was healthy and grateful for what I had been given.

During my twelve-month recovery my diet consisted of warm chicken broth, Jell-O, tepid mashed potatoes, etc., — anything soft and nourishing. It was the Snyder family who made sure that I was nourished throughout my recovery. I was advised by my doctor not to try to sing.

In my apartment, I was alone. No mom, no family and no responsibility. My self-esteem and overall communication had been shattered. Since my kids didn't have much to do with me since the divorce, they weren't a part of my cancer and recovery.

One day, my landlady came to visit to see how I was feeling. I invited her in and she handed me a Doug Oldham CD. She said, "I think this will help lift your spirits. The man is a gospel singer who has a wonderful and unique way of communicating the message of the Lord." She smiled with pride. "You know, when I was seventeen, he hired me to be his pianist."

After she left, I listened to his music and continued to listen to it every day. It was refreshing and uplifting to hear music that was free of a metronome. Doug Oldham's unique style made the message come alive.

Without distractions or a hectic schedule to adhere to, my time was spent alone with my thoughts. I had a sense of peace knowing that the boss upstairs had something in store for me. And, there was a reason why this was happening.

I didn't choose to have cancer, it chose me. For the first time in my life, I wasn't in control. However, I was in control of my attitude towards the cancer. I had to be in a positive frame of mind in order to allow the forces to work on my behalf. When I would drive to the local bookstores, I was drawn to literature on spiritual health and positive thinking. These books helped redirect my inner voice to not allow feelings of anger and a poor-me attitude govern my life. I accepted that I was powerless on my own.

To empower my ability to reprogram my way of thinking, I began to make an effort to do at least one nice thing for another person each day. I read once, that everyone has 86,400 seconds in a given day.

It makes you wonder how many people take a few seconds out of their hectic lives to say, "Thank you," or, do something kind for someone else.

I started every day with a feeling of gratitude. I found that when I focused on everything I was grateful for, it shifted my mind set off of feelings of scarcity, anguish and depression. Everything happens in life for a reason. When I found myself dealing with the absence of love, or the inability to attract what I desired, I had to look at how I was attracting these circumstances into my life. I realized that I could not solve a problem by condemning it. If I didn't like something, I had to change the way I looked at it.

At night, before going to sleep, I started to read the Bible. I truly believed that things were going to work out the way they were meant to be. Everything has a time and place.

Since the radiation destroyed the blood vessels to my vocal cord, full restoration after treatment was not possible. My vocal training enabled me to effectively use one chord to sing. Although, my voice tired easy, I was grateful to be alive.

After my year of recovery, I returned to the choir and slowly worked toward two hour rehearsals. When I was finally able to sing a solo, it was different. This time around, I sang from the heart. The accompanist would follow my phrasing so that the congregation received the message I wanted to convey.

I was in a different place and time in my life, a place that was quiet so that I could hear and feel the Lord's presence in and around me.

Lance A. McKay, Louis A. Mckay Jr.,
Louis A. Mckay Sr. Lita,A. Mckay,
Bradford D. Mckay

CHAPTER 19 – My Divorce And Consequences

One afternoon, my son Louis Jr., and I suggested that we meet for lunch. We talked for a long time. I had the opportunity to tell my side of the story. The differences that Joyce and I had should have never involved the kids, but it did. Now that he was a father and going through a divorce himself, he used my marriage as a gauge of what not to do. He voiced that the divorce split our family apart and that I should have made an effort to contact my kids and seen to it that our relationship stayed on track.

I felt that if the kids wanted something to do with me, they could have made the effort too. I've never been one to seek out other people and phone them to have something to do with me. I steer away from conflict.

He explained that Joyce felt insecure and if the kids had something to do with me, they were taking sides. Louis phoned Lance and I met with the both of them and soon I met with Brad and then eventually, Lisa.

One evening, I phoned Lita and invited her and her husband out for dinner. We talked for quite a long time, but I could tell that she was uncomfortable. However, I explained that there are two sides to every story and that losing our house and apartment in Banker's Hill was still raw and it didn't have to end the way it did. She felt that I could have made an effort to see her and I felt she could have made an effort to see me.

Years later, Louis, Jr., made the move and invited me over for holidays. Joyce and the rest of the family would be there and we managed to remain civil.

One afternoon, during a Labor Day Celebration, the family got into an altercation over religion. One thing led to another and words were said.

One side thought that the other should apologize and the other felt they deserved the apology. The two sides never met and the family was split once again.

It would be several years before I would see Lance and his family again. They would invite me up to their home for several church fish fry's, and 4th of July parties. I wouldn't stay long but I would make an appearance.

Lisa eventually would join Lance and Michelle for their holidays. However, the rest of the family did not communicate with them.

Louis, Jr., invited me over for Thanksgiving and holiday
BBQ's. I began to see the family more and the communication
and interaction between Joyce and I became amicable.

One afternoon while reading the DOUGLAS DAILY
DISPATCH, I noticed an announcement for the Cancer Relay for
Life. Douglas Arizona was to host the event at the Douglas
High School baseball field. Neighboring cities in southern
Arizona participated. Now that I was a throat cancer survivor,
the first year I volunteered, I was asked to sing for the opening
ceremony to start the 24-hour walkathon. Participants could
commute to and from their residence, pitch their pup-tents, or
stay at local hotels.

The relay begins on Saturday at 10 a.m. and ended at 10 a.m.
the following day. Money raised for this event is forwarded to
the American Cancer Society. Participants are volunteers, those
who walk, and those individuals or business' that contribute
financially. Volunteers fill a paper lunch bag with sand, place a
candle inside, and write the name of each donor on the outside
of the bag.

The bag is then placed around the baseball field. In the
evening, the volunteers light all the candles and the field lights

are turned off. Over the PA system, every name is read out loud to acknowledge and thank each person for their time, effort and participation. It warms my heart to know that I contribute to this worthy cause. I drive 1,150 miles round trip to Douglas each year.

As I approach the drive into the valley, between Benson and Bisbee, the beautiful sunset, with its breathtaking shades of red, yellow and purple, seems to envelope the four corners of my path. It's an eerie feeling that leaves me in awe.

The Saguaro and Prickly Pear Cactus add a unique splash of color during my desert trip.

I chuckle every time I pass the area where our car overheated in the dead of summer when I was a little boy. When I reach the top of the mountain, where Bisbee begins, I call Roy Manley, my baseball teammate, to let him know I'm thirty minutes out of Douglas and to meet me at the Hotel Gadsden.

The hotel staff is friendly and accommodating. Whenever I come to town, I order my favorite dish - Chorizo and Eggs. The cook makes it special for me; eggs over-easy, chorizo and beans separate from each other on fresh, warm flour tortillas. To top it off, I order a glass of ice-cold draft Budweiser.

My mother taught me that if you add a pinch of salt on the top of your beer the alcohol will not go to your head.

When I arrive at the Gadsden, Roy is sitting on the bench outside, waiting with his Polaroid camera. As I open the doors to the lobby, Roy takes a picture once I say, "I'm home." We have dinner, reminisce and laugh. He's such a great story-teller. At times, we laughed so hard, our eyes watered. He's such a historian. He knows everything there is to know about Arizona.

The next day, I would meet another baseball teammate, Albert Jordan, nicknamed, "Beto." Roy, Albert and I would have lunch at the Gadsden. Later that evening, another baseball teammate, Robert Aguilar and his son, would drive 100 miles, from Sierra Vista, to have dinner with all of us. We made it a point to drive to Agua Prieta, in Sonora, Mexico for a haircuts. Times have changed. Now, we need to bring our passports.

The day of the Cancer Relay Event, the minister gives his message and I sing two songs; Listen to the Hammer Ring, "I Walked Today, and "Where Jesus Walked."

On Sunday, it was time to head home to San Diego. I love to visit Douglas. However, I don't think I could ever live there. In San Diego, everything I need is within a twenty minute car-ride from my apartment. Most importantly, the deciding factor is that the closest VA Hospital to Douglas is a 129 mile drive to Tucson, AZ.

On the way back, I always stop in Bisbee to have lunch with my cousin, Sergio Lopez at the Country Club in Naco, AZ.

I always stop and admire the wonderful little town of Bisbee. The Copper Queen still stands in excellent condition. There are only two roads; one to enter and one to exit. The town is very artsy — buildings painted different colors and stairs everywhere. Since the homes are built into the sides of the mountain, residents have to climb stairs in order to reach their homes. The town hosts the "Bisbee 1000," — an event where participants of all ages and from all over the city climb 1000 stairs in October of every year, to benefit the cancer drive. The towns bustles with artists, bird conservatories and quilt makers. Its common to see individuals painting on the streets or walking around with birds on their shoulders.

In November of every year, Douglas also holds a ceremony acknowledging veterans who fought in our foreign wars. The first time I attended, I was invited to sing, "It Has Always Been A Soldier." The song is about a soldier who makes a sacrifice for his country. Since it's quite a drive to Douglas, I now make one trip and that is for The Cancer Relay for life.

It's important for me to keep in touch with my hometown. I contribute to the on-going restoration of the Grand Theatre. The people of Douglas don't care what you do for a living, where you live, how you live, or what you drive. They care if you care. They're too busy living their own lives.

In my day, the population of Douglas was 8,000 people. We had football, basketball, and baseball. Today, there are over 16,000 people and growing steadily. Every sport imaginable, and every educational resource, and scholarship programs is available to the community and to the young people of Douglas.

There are many bake-sales and dances to help raise money and support the Historical Society and the Grand Theatre renovation. There is also an organization from California called The Douglas Arizona Social Club. These members originate from the Douglas area. They raise funds by hosting 4 dances a

My old teammates, Roy Manley and
Albert(Beto) Jordan

I attend the Cancer Society's Relay for Life as well as Douglas High School Alumni reunions. Here I am with Roy Manley and Albert Jordan. (McKay family photo.)

year in Springfield, California. With the proceeds from selling raffle tickets, the members travel by bus to Douglas and give educational scholarships to deserving high school seniors.

Today, students have scholarships, tutoring and after school programs. Areas of town that were either open fields are now abundant with homes and communities.

Not having these opportunities available in my day, may have been the catalyst that helped drive me to seek opportunities to better my life, despite the obstacles that surfaced.

CHAPTER 20 – Marines Presentation Plaque And Metal

In 2006, I was invited to attend the Bells of Freedom at
Camp Pendleton in Oceanside, CA. Louis, Jr., and his wife
Tanya own Bells of Freedom a non-profit organization.
Teachers, students, and families from their dance studio North
CountyDance Arts, Inc. and various businesses, provide
Christmas to battalions stationed at Camp Pendleton – either
awaiting deployment or whose spouse has already been
deployed.

The holiday gift baskets include gift certificates and fixings
for a holiday dinner, gift cards for each parent and gifts of each
child's wish-list. These families are stationed at Camp
Pendleton in Oceanside, CA.

This particular year, The Chaplin on base gathered the
families inside the chapel for a prayer and a moment of thanks
and recognition. The base colonel asked me to come up to the
front. He presented me with a handcrafted cultured marble
plaque bearing The Marine Corps Hymn engraved over the
Marine Emblem. Also engraved, are depictions of air support as
marine platoons invade a beach head. All of this is beautifully
encased in a mahogany frame. I looked up with tears in my eyes

as the marines stood at attention and saluted. I turned the frame around and on the back was handwritten: **To Louis A. McKay, Sr. In appreciation of your contributions to the Corps and Country: Presented by the Marines and families of the Assault Amphibian School Battalion. Semper Fiddles (Forever Faithful).** I asked the women and children to stand, and, said, "You are why we win wars. Without your support and love, we couldn't have survived."

The Colonel also presented me with an Assault Amphibious School Battalion Pocket Medal. On the back of the medal, are engraved amphibious Amtracs carrying marines onto a beach head where the Japanese are defending themselves against our attack. The front reads: Department of the Navy – United States Marine Corps. According to the Colonel, a marine carries this for life. He said, "When a marine is on liberty, and out drinking with his buddies, he should always make sure he has his medal in his pocket. When the bill arrives, each marine pulls out their medal and lays it on the table. The guy who forgot his would pay the entire bill or splits it with the others who also forgot theirs."

In early 2007, I drove my daughter, Lita, to an appointment and waited across the street at a restaurant to get a bite to eat. During my meal, I felt a weakness in my left arm. I paid my bill and asked a young man to help me to my car. I drove across the street and waited for my daughter.

When Lita finished her appointment, she walked around to the driver's side and noticed that I was sitting with my legs facing outward. Right away, she asked if I was feeling okay. I felt fine. However, my artificial leg was not responding as it should. For some reason, it was difficult to maneuver. I told her it does this when it needs to be adjusted. I promised her that I would make an appointment as soon I returned to my apartment. I drove her home and on the way to the post office, the weakness persisted. I couldn't get out of my car, so I asked a lady to retrieve the mail and bring it to my car. I drove to my apartment but couldn't move my left leg to get out of the car. Fortunately, a maintenance man was working in the garage. I asked him to call 911.

I didn't know what was happening. Paramedics arrived and transported me to Sharp Memorial Hospital. The Veteran's Hospital didn't have a bed available. Tests soon revealed a TIA or mini-stroke, caused by a blood clot in my neck. With this type of stroke, there is seldom a residual effect. It can take quite awhile before your strength is restored. Doctors kept me over-night for observation. However, I ended up staying about a week in the hospital. They recommended physical therapy to get my strength back and suggested a nursing facility.

Although I enjoy my independence and my apartment is in close proximity to the bank, post office, or grocery stores, I accepted that I couldn't be alone due to my unsteadiness. I had a choice of either staying at a nursing facility or staying with family.

Lita phoned Joyce and explained the situation. She offered her spare bedroom which had a private bath and shower. This way, each could have their privacy.

For me, it was an easy decision to make. The nurse and physical therapist could come over and someone would oversee my progress and be with me throughout the day and night. Once I settled in at Joyce's I began using a walker and soon graduated to a cane. In the beginning, things were strained and we didn't have any problem telling each other where to head off. In time, Joyce and I would take walks in the evening to the end of the block. My son, Brad, would drop by on his way home and massage my legs and body so that I could relax. My other son, Louis Jr., come over and adjusted my neck and back. My son in-law Luis would run my daily errands to the post office, bank and mail my bills so that I could keep current with my obligations. I later found out that Joyce would come to my bedroom and check on me to make sure I was breathing. She said it was the first time in her life she didn't hear me snore.

She prepared my breakfast every morning and made sure I ate three meals a day. I gained a little weight staying at Joyce's, but, I didn't care. I enjoyed her company, the attention and her wonderful cooking. She saw to it that I did my daily exercises using one of her antique wooden chairs in the dining room. Once I regained my strength and received a clearance from my doctor stating that I could drive, I moved back to my apartment.

However, Joyce and I continued to have dinner together. Joyce took care of me and nursed me back to health. For that, I will be eternally grateful.

For the first time, we were able to date without children. We would sit and discuss the problems of the world. In the afternoon, we would sit at the kitchen table and watch the birds, squirrels, doves, and hummingbirds come for their daily visit at the feeders. Hummingbirds were so attracted to her feeder they would hover in air, waiting for their chance to eat. It was such a joy to see.

The squirrels couldn't be cuter. Joyce and I would sit and laugh at the amount of food the squirrels could fit in their little jaws. A 50-pound bag of wild bird seed would last maybe three weeks at best. You never could be sure, because it all depended on the amount of new animals. We would sit in awe and watch all of the animals eat together.

Friday's we set aside for Joyce. She had a standing hair appointment. Lita had taken her for a number of years. However, I wanted to take over that responsibility. She scheduled her nail appointments and on the way home, we would grocery shop. Imagine that, Joyce and I enjoying grocery shopping. Employees would help us with fresh bread, food samples, or really anything we wanted for that matter. If Joyce asked for it, she'd get it. The fact that she was nice about it played a role in how people treated her. She never wanted to go anywhere unless her hair was done. I would come by and pick her up, drop her off, and if she gave me a kiss, I'd give her a check for whatever appointment she was going to.

She'd say, "Go into that vault or wallet of yours and just give me the cash." I later found out that she would write a check to her self and keep the cash. I so enjoyed our time together. At times, we'd fill up the shopping cart, and then when we reached the cashier and unloaded the groceries, she'd smile and pull out her Von's card and say, "What are you waiting on?" Joyce would always go to the same cashier, every Friday. When we got home, we'd have cocktails and dinner. During the week, we would watch, "Dr. Phil," "Oprah,""Judge Judy," "Two and a Half Men," and "Dancing with the Stars."

During a Padre baseball game, she'd get real upset when we lost. She'd say, "We just farted and fell." "It's a dirty shame, to play like we did and lose." "We'd be lost without our short-stop – Kahlil Green." However, when we did win, she'd say, "We won by the skin of our teeth." She'd also be frustrated with the San Diego Chargers.

As soon as weather permitted, she'd want to be outside on her deck. In the mornings, she'd enjoy her coffee, and in the evenings, her glass of white wine or champagne. If I got chilly, she'd bring me a blanket or a hooded sweatshirt so we could be together and have a cocktail. I had a chance to enjoy the family again with Joyce. She'd cook these wonderful meals with whatever she had on hand. Her soups, casseroles, roasts, fried chicken, chicken-fried steak, meatloaf, and bean soup were the best. She just had a way of seasoning that was unique to her. When family would come over and visit, and have dinner, we'd laugh like old times. There was a sense of togetherness that had been missing for many years.

I had noticed that she was beginning to tell people (including me) her true feelings instead of hiding them. If it meant that she let you have it, you pushed her to that point. She didn't want to have anything or anyone around her that was going to make her unhappy.

One day, during one of our visits, Joyce complained about a pain in her neck and a headache. I went to the store and purchased some Aleve. The pain got better but never went away. She had started to leave dishes in the sink saying, "I can do them in the morning." I thought for once she's going to relax. We would laugh when she would open the refrigerator and forget what she went there to get. We'd laugh because we're 84 years-old and its o.k.

The day before Thanksgiving, Lita came over to help prep. She didn't know it, but I had already pulled apart all of the bread. I wanted to help. Lita opened up a bottle Champagne, and we prepped for turkey day. All of us laughed continuously the entire day at the simplest things, from Joyce forgetting how much of a particular seasoning she put in to not being able to read the recipe when Lita asked how she made her infamous Pumpkin Chiffon pie. The cranberry jello recipe Joyce brought from Kansas had to have the hot and cold water added at a specific time, or it wouldn't come out right. Seeing Joyce laugh with Lita was a wonderful sight.

The week after Thanksgiving, Lita came over and put up her tree and Joyce sang and danced throughout the house. When she would hand Lita the white bear from Linda to top the tree, they reminisced about how much they missed her. She was so eager and happy to get the tree decorated. This was the earliest that the tree had ever been decorated. She had said, "I just want my tree up, I don't care about anything else."

The next day, I came over for dinner, and the house had been transformed into Christmas. That evening, Joyce appeared tired. She was scheduled to go over her lab results with her doctor in a few weeks, so she didn't pay attention to how she was feeling. During our visits, she'd say, "I just don't know why I feel so tired. I haven't done much."

In all the years I've known Joyce, she never complained of feeling overwhelmed. In a few days, Lita and Luis came over for dinner and finished decorating the outside. Now, Joyce was going to have the entire month of December to enjoy her decorations. Luis and Lita would come over and join us for dinner and cocktails and Joyce would have her music playing and sing to her heart's content. At 84, she could still hit a high C. Other evenings, Joyce and I would sit in the front room by the fire and listen to Tony Bennett, KD Lang, and a host of other singers.

This Christmas Eve, she wanted to prepare something different other than the traditional prime-rib. She phoned Louis Jr., asked him what he would like to have. He requested the family favorite - Chicken Fried Steak, mash potatoes and gravy.

There were only 12 people coming over, so this was going to be an easier year than usual.

During the evening, I could tell something was odd. Joyce was not herself. Having the amount of people walk in and out of the kitchen and the stove close to the entrance, it was very easy for one's body to touch the temperature on the oven knob. When it came time to take the steak out of the oven, the temperature was over 300 degrees. The meat was over cooked and in Joyce's eyes, her meal was ruined.

Later, as the family sat around the tree and listened to El Divo sing "Ave Maria." I asked Joyce to sing like she did the other night while decorating. She looked at me, and said, "Not tonight, I'll sing for you another time." This stunned both Lita and I because if anyone would sing at the drop of a hat, it was Joyce.

When everyone had left, it took but a second before Joyce said, "I'm done and I'm going to bed." The next evening, Lita invited us over for a little get together. I picked up Joyce and we drove over. She didn't feel like going, but didn't want to hurt Lita's feelings. We had a nice time, but Joyce felt tired and we left early.

When I phoned Joyce the next day to let her know I was on my way over for our cocktail hour, Lita answered the phone. She said to come to the house. When I arrived, Paramedics and the Fire Department were parked in front. Joyce had collapsed and fell to the floor. She had called Lita because she didn't remember falling. On the way to UCSD, Joyce had multiple seizures. Tests revealed a mass on her lungs and 14 lesions on the brain. She didn't have a family history of lung cancer, never smoked a day in her life, and lived a healthy lifestyle.

Unfortunately, her condition worsened; both lungs collapsed and she had pneumonia and was put on a ventilator and a feeding tube.

Lita phoned Louis Jr., away as he had just arrived in Utah. When the doctors came out during the call, Louis Jr., asked Lita if Joyce had a directive, Lita told Louis to get home as fast as he could.

Unfortunately, there were no flights available out of Utah until the next day, so they rented a car. Everyone in the family was notified of Joyce's condition. Lisa phoned Lance. It had been about 10 years since the family had seen Lance. He arrived at the hospital and kept a vigil along with the rest of the family. When Joyce's condition stabilized, she was transferred to Grossmont Hospital in La Mesa where specialists were summoned. When Joyce's ventilator and feeding tube were finally removed, Lance and Michelle were at her bedside with their boys. She wanted the brothers to make amends and for her family to be together again.

Tests revealed malignant lung cancer that had spread to the brain. At best, she had a few months to live. Since she never regained use of her upper left side and was unable to sit up on her own, radiation therapy was not an option.

Joyce lasted a total of 31 days in the hospital. I was at her bedside daily. One day, Lita was holding her hand. She asked, "Where's dad?" I spoke up and said, "I'm right here. I'll be here for you every day. I love you." She said, "I love you too."

She didn't like all the liquids she had to drink and hated the taste of Ensure. She would say, "Get me out of here."

One day, we laughed when she asked me what doctors came to check on her. Trying to hold back a smile, I told her he was our Pediatrician and that we're going to have more kids. She said, "Oh crap! You are out of your mind."

During Joyce's stay at the hospital, the nurses would compliment her beautiful skin. Family relatives, kids, grandkids and friends treasured their time spent with Joyce.

One day, a weekend nurse misread a doctor's order and stopped a medication. This mistake made Joyce lethargic and she never was able to speak again. To us, we felt robbed of precious time.

Within the week, Joyce's body was beginning to shut down. She was transferred to Lakeview Home (a hospice house in coordination with Grossmont Hospital). That evening, we had a torrential rain fall. At 5:00 a.m. the next morning, Lita received a call that Joyce had taken a turn for the worse. She passed away at 6:08 a.m. Her passing was very peaceful.

The family planned her memorial at University Christian Church, in San Diego, California. The choir sang, "The Sparrow," in honor of Joyce. It was the most beautiful service I have ever seen. People in attendance said they had never experienced such a joyous and emotional service.

Joyce had always respected the Marine Corps uniform. During Joyce's stay at the hospital, Sgt. Major and the commander of the Marines at Camp Pendleton often inquired about her condition. When Louis Jr., told the commander that Joyce had passed away, they were devastated and wanted to do something. Since Joyce had always respected the military and was always part of the military exchange program. Louis Jr.said, "There is one thing that would mean the world to my mom and our entire family, a Marine Colour Guard." The commander said, "You got it." This is no small feat!

A full Colour Guard with military honors marched in their "Dress Blues." They were holding the American flag, the Marine flag, two soldiers were on each side holding rifles, and two soldiers holding swords. As they marched into the church, everyone was in awe and tears flowed down their cheeks. This ceremony is so special that it is reserved only for the military and the military elite. At the end of the memorial service, the military walked in and saluted Joyce.

Unbeknownst to the family, I arranged to have the service recorded. When I was given the tapes, I then took them to Art Jenesta, grandson to the late Mrs. Josephine Bergner, so that he could make a CD. I've kept in contact with his family throughout the years, so when it came time to have this done, Art was the right choice.

Unfortunately, the tape where all of the kids reminisced about their childhood and the love of their mother was lost. To this day, it has never been found at Art's home or mine.

Life without Joyce is empty. My daughter Lita refreshes Joyce's handkerchiefs with her "White Diamonds," so that I can keep her fragrance with me. I keep it in a zip-lock bag, tucked away in the side pocket of my jacket.

The following year, the day before Mother's Day, all the kids gathered at Joyce's favorite place, Julian, CA. We had a wonderful dinner at Julian Grille and stayed the night at the Julian Lodge. The next morning we enjoyed a nice breakfast. Lisa and her boys had purchased two fruitless plum trees and Lance and his wife, Michelle, had already chosen the perfect place to plant the trees. The family wanted to have Joyce live on. We chose to add her ashes to the soil when the boys were planting and then gave each person and handful to spread themselves.

When the estate company found the recording of Joyce singing "Ave Maria," "The Lord's Prayer," and a church hymn, everyone was elated. This meant that we could hear her voice whenever we wanted. Since the record was old and scratched,

Lance took it to a music studio to have it digitally mastered. Lance had the studio copy all of the songs onto a CD for each of us. It played as we planted the trees in Julian.

As I glanced around at the family working together, it was as if Joyce's death brought the family back together. Today, we all make an effort to stay in touch and treasure our time together. Holidays are different without Joyce. It feels like all make an effort to stay in touch and treasure our time together. Father's day is spent on the golf course with Lance, Louis, Jr., and their sons. Lita and I follow along in our golf cart. We toast with some Tequila and spend the first part of the day together. Lance and Michelle have an Easter dinner outside by their pool and have a 4th of July BBQ. They rotate Thanksgiving and Christmas with Louis and Tanya. Luis and Lita have birthday dinners and an annual Christmas party. The brothers and sisters get together once a week for dinner. And it helps to reinforce that they are family, good, bad or indifferent.

I contacted Cissy's cousin and found out that she died of a heart attack while in Germany when she was in her early 40's. She was buried in Los Angeles. Her daughter contacted me and mentioned that she had heard about me from her mother and said that I held a very special place in her heart.

My school buddies and I keep in contact and enjoy each other's company when I visit Douglas. Unfortunately, Robert Aguilar passed away in 2010 and Herman Simon in 2011. Ron Manley, my Douglas historian and Albert Jordon are alive and well and reside in Douglas.

Wilford invited me up to Fullerton, CA, for a Flag Day presentation at the Fullerton Elks, Lodge 1493, and to talk about my experiences in World War II, and about going with him to Washington DC with the San Diego Honor Flight.

CHAPTER 21-When the Opportunity Presents Itself, Embrace it with All Your Heart and Soul

I have come to believe that when you take the time to embrace nature at work, you see God's beauty. Every day, I thank him for another day. At 92 years of age, I have the time to observe, enjoy, and to love. Everyone has the opportunity to take the time to enjoy life as its given.

In my family, my kids knew that Sundays were family day. After I drove the family to church, we either went out to eat, or came home to have a wonderful Sunday dinner. Evenings were spent watching, "The Wonderful World of Disney," or "Mutual of Omaha's Wild Kingdom," or other family programs that were on TV. My point is that we were together as a family. You have to make the time because you feel it's important. When you're there, be there. When the opportunity presents itself, embrace it with all your heart and soul. Don't wait until you're in your 80's.

I am proud to be a marine, and in my heart, I will always be one. The mindset of a marine back when I was fighting is one of a trained killer — one that protects one's country, family, and children. Like I've mentioned before, it's a mindset of "Kill or be killed".

Today, our country is at war fighting against an entity that wants to annihilate the western civilization. The United States has a tough battle to fight. In my day, wars were fought differently. I can't speak for the other branches of the military. When our country was fighting against the enemy, the marine was not there to negotiate or aid in an occupational force — they were there to annihilate the enemy. Innocent children and citizens will die. This is the cost of war.

Religion, money, and politics have been around since the beginning of time. History has proven that these catalysts are just as prevalent today as they were in biblical times. I believe religion, money, politics, and conflict are beneficial to the masses, only when they are used to appease the ego, do they get out of control.

Politics have continued through the centuries as a vehicle of influence. Money has always been an instrument of persuasion and conflict, and always will be the result of an ego. We have to live in the NOW! Without the uncertainty of the future.

Living in the past robs the present of its reality. He who has a "why" to live for, can bear almost anything. The more I let go of myself, and my ego, the more spiritually fulfilled I become.

The attitude we take when we give to another is crucial. Give because it is the right thing to do, not for what you will receive in return. When you truly give of yourself, you experience goodness, truth, and beauty.

Being unloved is a tragedy. By loving another human being, you transform a tragedy into a triumph. In order to change a predicament into an achievement, one must change their attitude. Many times, I've allowed myself to be broken by what has happened in the past. Use your past as a guide and realize that the potential has been actualized, the meaning fulfilled, the value realized. It cannot be removed by anyone or anything.

Too many people are self-serving, shoving their impatience on others and not listening to their inner voice. They think that if they try harder to fit a round peg into a square hole, they will be happy. This is not the case. What is to be, already is? I have found that when you are of service to others, you are connected to a higher source something far greater than your body, mind or **Ego**!

My mother's trunk provided me an opportunity to reflect on my life as a young boy, a son, a brother. an athlete, a man, a soldier, a husband, a father, a grand-father, and a great-grandfather. My voice throughout my life has been one of determination, hard work, pain, triumph, anger and forgiveness.

My hope is that my story will inspire others to persevere — to focus on the possible rather than the impossible, and to be in state of gratitude for everything in your life.

My mothers Metal Trunk

Louis A. McKay,Rose N. Cruz Clements, Wilma L.Cruz Miller, and Wilford Cruz

Wilford,Wilma, Rose, and Adolpho Cruz, came to visit me at the Naval Hospital in San Diego with Mom.

Left to right, Row 1 - Lillywhite, Rabago, Simon, Powles, M.Rochin, D. Jones, Jordan, Dodds,, Row 2 - Morales, Manley, Hoffman, Lorack, Ames, Brady, Carpenter, H. Cochin, Munson, Row 3 - J.Jones, Donaldson, Schultz, Hannum, Fields, Klutz, McKay,Cota

*Looking south on G. Avenue on the
foreground left The Grand Theatre,
Louis won a 1st place in a singing
contest. (a bust of President Franklin D.
Roosevelt) & The Hotel Gadsden where
Luisa Castillo met Louis's dad Alex Lou
Mckay which was owned by Louis'
Grandfather.*

211

Louis a crushing 143 pound fullback
Honorable Mention State Champion

Notice I've tackled the
opposing player so hard that
both our helmets are starting
to come off. (Copper Kettle

Notice I've tackled the opposing player
so hard that both our helmets are starting to come off. (Copper Kettle photo.)

Louis has carried his smile and friendliness onto the athletic field and displayed his sportsmanship and elsewhere in Douglas High School.

My first son, Army Paratrooper, E-7 Sgt.First Class Combat; Engineer, 82nd Airborne Nuclear Engineer ,Explosives, Drill Sgt. Bradford Douglas Mckay

213

I salute all men that have served in the military,
civilians, the folks at home,that kept the ammunition coming as
we made sure our enemies would never touch the homeland.

Louis McKay of North Park, one of the more, than one-hundred World War II veterans headed to Washington DC, Friday, as part of the Honor Flight San Diego trip to the World War II National Memorial in Washington DC on Saturday, reads a letter from his sister-in-law during mail call where the veterans received letters during the flight from San Diego. — Howard Lipin

Honor Flight San Diego is a non-profit team of volunteers escorting San Diego County Veterans to Washington DC World War II Memorial.

Louis Mckay Sr. Sisters,Rose N.
Clements, Wilma L.Miller, and Brother
Wilford Cruz, and Mom, Maria Luisa
Castillo, Mckay, Cruz

Louis visits Douglas every year for the Cancer Relay Fundraiser and reunites with this teammates Ray Manley,Robert Aguilar, and Albert (Beto)Jordan,"We have a great time and celebrate memories and our old friendships.

McKay grinding his teeth ready to tackle.

*Basketball Team,Louis #.36 and Coach
Sanset,Manley Row - 2nd Back far right.*

My Grandma
Enestelada Castillo

My Grandpa
Nicholas Castillo

WORLD WAR II MEMORIAL US
MARINE CORPS ,-WASHINGTON, .DC.
The Price of Freedom: The Freedom Wall
holds 4,048 gold stars. Each gold star
represents one hundred American service
personnel who died or remain missing in
the war. The 405,399 American Dead and
missing from World War II are second
only to the loss of more than 620,000
Americans during the Civil War. My next
stop was to be, Iwo Jima, but was put on
hold when I was wounded in Okinawa and
lost my leg below my knee.

On my trip to Washington DC Memorial, I visited the Lincoln Monument. My niece Colleen Cruz stood behind me and watched me as I turned by head upward. I took her hand and placed it on my cheek, as a tear had brought wetness and asked her if she felt it? She said, "Yes." That was the first tear I have shed since the war. I told her, I just couldn't do it. It was a hell of a thing. I was blown to bits. But I lived. And they were better men. They deserved to be here. I didn't. But, I am grateful that I am. She asked me, "if I had ever regretted going to war, or enlisting in the Marines?" I told her I lost my friends, my fiancee, my livelihood, and my leg. I told her never once, I knew where I was needed. I tightened my laces and went. My only regret I had, was that I didn't do more.

*I was wounded in Okinawa and could not
make it to Iwo Jima*

Swisha Marine Division 2, Mascot

My Purple Heart, Battlefield Medals,
Dog Tags,Honorable Discharge
Certificate

The mask of my mother that helped make me,
the man I am...I love my Mother!

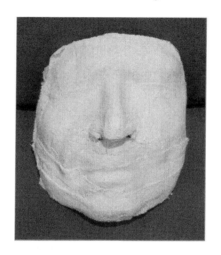

On liberty: Me on the left, a guy I don't remember, "Tiny," and my lifelong buddy Herman Simon. (McKay family photo.)

I am Left to right the 5th player No.3 in the Front Row

ACHIEVEMENT AWARDS

State Board of Cosmetology – March 12, 1949

Silver Anniversary Convention for Hairstyling –

1st Place 1954

Long Beach Hairdressers Guild Hair Styling

Award, February 18, 1951

Louis McKay – President - San Diego Hair

Styling Panel

Empire University "Beauty Culture" Los

Angeles, CA

Hairdresser and Cosmetician Diploma January

28, 1949

Hollywood College of Beauty, Hollywood,

California,CA, Diploma Advanced Hairstyling,

September 11, 1958

San Diego Hairstyling Panel – Member 1951

Miss Teen Pageant – Certificate of Appreciation

Gracias Por Su Ayuda – La Estudientina de

Azulan 1977-78

*Supervised students in the beauty school to
compete and improve their technique.*
San Diego Hair Styling panel – President
1958-59

Hollywood Hair Design Council Appreciation
Award – Congress of Beauty Show 1961
Joanie Golden Angel Award – 1986
Clairol – 1st Place Coloring Contest
Angel Victory Award for the Music and
Performing Arts Angels
1st Talent Award – SDCCA 1961 NBSW
(National Beauty Salon Week)
State of California Commission of Teacher
Credentialing – Music Clear Single Subject –
June 1, 1995 – June 1, 2000
Spanish Bilingual Cross-Culture Education –
June   1 1995-June 1 2000
University of San Diego – Graduate Division –
Master's Degree in Education - August 31, 1980
Starlight Star Award – Outstanding Male
Performance in a comedy role — "Sitting Bull"&
"Annie Get Your Gun"
1st Place for the Sister Rossi Competition
USD

Starlight Award of Merit 1974

Grand Theatre – Douglas Arizona – Singing
Award

Miss Teen Pageant – Certificate of Appreciation

Gracias Por Su Ayuda – La Estudientina de
Azulan 1977-78

1st Talent Award – SDCCA 1961 NBSW
(National Beauty Salon Week)

Hollywood Coiffure Guild - Oscar 1st Place -
1952 – Permanent Waving

CHFC 1962 – Artistry in Hair Design

Roberta Tate – Advanced Hairstyling Award for
Outstanding Ability in Hair Design

Chairman – NBSW (National Beauty Salon
Week) Appreciation Award from San Diego
County Cosmetologist

San Diego Hairstyling Panel – Member

Hollywood Hair Design Council – Judge for
International Hairstyling in San Francisco

Diego Cosmetologist Unit 20--President
1962-63 University of San Diego – Bachelor of
Arts Degree in Music May 21, 1978
State of California Commission of Teacher
Credentialing – Music Clear Single Subject –
June 1, 1995 – June 1, 2000
Spanish Bilingual Cross-Culture Education –
June   1 1995-June 1 2000
University of San Diego – Graduate Division –
Master's Degree in Education, August 31, 1980
Starlight Star Award – Outstanding Male
Performance in a comedy role — "Sitting Bull"&
"Annie Get Your Gun"
1st Place for the Sister Rossi Competition
USD
Starlight Award of Merit 1974
Grand Theatre – Douglas Arizona – Singing
Award
Miss Clairol Competition for Hair Coloring
Chairman El Cortez Hotel, San Diego, Ca.

Voice Teacher for Professional Technique

1995-2000

Hairstylist for the crowning of Beauties past 70,

Chairman, San Diego County Cosmetologist

Current Member of "American Guild of Musical

Artist of New York"

Current Members of "Opera America" Singer and

Teacher for the state of California

Life Member of the Douglas Arizona Historical

Society

Alumni Choir Member – First Presbyterian

Reunion Concert November 12, 2006

Current Active Choir Member of University

Christian Church, San Diego, CA.

Mom's reminder that she had a Marine
fighting, WWII, and was constantly
praying, for my return, safe and sound.
Thanks mom, I miss you. Love your son.

53396864R00129

Made in the USA
Charleston, SC
08 March 2016